"*Relationships with others are the physical and spiritual basis of creative energy. Nothing is further from the truth than the popular notion that we create alone and in isolation from the world.*" *Shaun McNiff*

WHAT OTHERS ARE SAYING

"*I love the concept of women gathering together to nurture their creativity. This offers a double dose of benefits – community and camaraderie AND support for creativity, both so essential to our wellbeing. Too often we ignore our creative stirrings. I hope lots of women are inspired by this terrific idea for a club.*"
Marla Paul author: The Friendship Crisis

"*Just thinking each month about what I can do creatively has transformed my life. Most importantly, I met fabulous women! When I tell others about our creativity club they are in awe and love the idea. They wish they had something like this in their lives.* " *Patricia O'Connor, Life Coach, ChFc*

"*I love the support, energy, and enthusiasm of women sharing their lives and cheering one another on at our monthly creativity meetings. I love witnessing and being witnessed. Our creativity club has made my life fuller and given me a feeling of friendship and unconditional lovingness.*"
Judy Wolf Writer & Life Adventurer

"*I just LOVE my creativity group! Creativity seems to be the "glue" or the focal point for unfolding who we are. It's a safe place to share whatever we create, think, feel.*" *Barb Trevvett, Retired LMFT*

"*Our creativity club meeting on the second Wednesday of each month is a holy day of obligation for me! It is built into my calendar. I feel like a thirst has been quenched. I begin to look forward to our meetings the very morning after we've just met. The network of women is an incredible gift of the highest good*"!
Nancy Zumpano High school Math teacher

"*Our monthly creativity group? This is my church!*"
Jan Ferris, LCSWR

THE CREATIVITY & CAMARADERIE CLUB HANDBOOK

HAVE MORE FUN
LIVE MORE WHOLEHEARTEDLY
ENCOURAGE EACH OTHER

MARY REILLY MATHEWS, LCSWR

DANU PRESS

CLINTON, NEW YORK

Cover Design: Derek Murphy: www.bookcovers.creativindie.com
Logo design and image preparation: www.HaileFinePhotography. com

Danu Press Ordering Information:
Quantity sales. Special discounts are available on quantity purchases by corporations, associations, and others. For details, contact:
www.danupress.com/

CONTENTS

Foreword 1

A Simple Idea, A Big Effect 3
What Started it All 5
Will Anyone Want to Do This With Me? 7
The Hunger for Meaningful Community.......................9
Ten Benefits of a Creativity & Camaraderie Club 11
Better than a Book Club?.. 15
But is This Selfish? 17

A Flexible and Generous Definition of Creativity 19
The Six Arenas for Creative Wholehearted Living 23
Prioritize Process Over Product.................................... 28
Welcoming all Stages of the Creative Cycle 29
The Creative Cycle 29

Gather Your Allies..33
Where to Find Likely Candidates.................................35
First Find an Ally...36
Good Candidates 38
People to Avoid 39
The Invitation 41

The Structure That Holds it All Together 45
How to Be a Compassionate Witness...........................52
Checklist for Co-Founders of a Creativity & Camaraderie
Club.. 55
The Time Keeper's Job..59

Seven Guiding Qualities of a Successful Creativity &
Camaraderie Club...60

Pot-Luckier Fun... 63

Developmental Phases of a Group........................... 67
What to Expect as Your Group Matures 69
Stages of Group Development.................................. 69

Protecting Group Boundaries 77
Twelve Sure-Fire Ways to Sabotage Group Success and
Longevity (the "Kisses of Death"): 79

The Ripple Effect of Creative Living 81
Responding to Outside Interest and Enthusiasm 86

Jumpstarting a More Creative Life 89
Dare to Dabble, Dabble to Dare 91
Questions to Get You Going 93
Note to Self: Rehearsing What You Truly Desire 96

Have More Fun, Live More Wholeheartedly, Encourage Each
Other.. 99

Appendix A: Resources 105
Appendix B: Creative Acts 115
Appendix C: Prompts.. 119
Appendix D: Sample Affirmations 121
Appendix E: Pot Luck Possibilities 123
Appendix F: Creativity Quotes 125

For my ancestors:
This is my offering in honor of you.

For my husband:
Our commitment has been the container that allows me to thrive.

For my children:
You are my greatest creation!

For all of our children's children:
May you participate joyfully in this creative universe.

Disclaimer

This book is designed to provide information on creating, fostering, and maintaining an ongoing creativity club group. It is sold with the understanding that the publisher and author are not engaged in rendering psychological, legal, or other professional services. If psychological, legal, or other expert assistance is required, the services of a competent professional should be sought.

Anyone who decides to gather people together must expect to invest some time and attention to maintain group structure, set and keep respectful boundaries, and enforce the group guidelines. Every effort has been made to make this manual as complete and as accurate as possible; however, there may be situations that arise in your group that are not anticipated in this manual. Therefore, this text should be used only as a general guide and not as the ultimate source on group dynamics. You are encouraged to explore other material, learn as much as possible about group dynamics and creativity, and tailor the information to your individual needs.

The purpose of this manual is to educate, encourage, and entertain. The author, and Danu Press, shall have neither liability nor responsibility to any person or entity with respect to any loss or damage caused, or alleged to have been caused, directly or indirectly, by the information contained in this book.

If you do not wish to be bound by the above, you may return this book to the publisher for a full refund.

Foreword

Mary Mathews generously shares her down-to-earth wisdom in this practical and inspirational guide on how to start a Creativity & Camaraderie Club. I first met Mary fourteen years ago, when she studied in our creativity and art therapy program. Back then she exuded enthusiasm and joy, cheering others on in their creative explorations. She has continued celebrating creativity all these years and now is supporting others to cheer as well.

Mary skillfully describes in detail how to begin and develop your own Creativity & Camaraderie Club. She draws on her extensive knowledge of human nature with guidance on:

- addressing your fears and concerns
- criteria for selecting members
- managing time
- developing guidelines for how to develop a safe, supportive environment.

So do yourself a favor. Read this book. Then start your own Creativity & Camaraderie Club. You'll be serving yourself and others. Your life will be rewarded in countless ways. How could you resist bringing more joy and fun into your life?

Yes, it takes some effort, but you don't have to do it alone. You'll have Mary expertly guiding you every step of the way.

Dale Schwarz, M. Ed. , ATR, LMHC

May 2013

Center for Creative Consciousness

Author: *Facilitative Coaching: A Toolkit for Expanding Your Repertoire and Achieving Lasting Results*

Playful printmaking has become a passion for Mary Mathews
Stand Tall trace monotype / ancient goddess series

1

A Simple Idea, A Big Effect

. . . May I be so bold as to offer you a gift?
If I may, read on. I gift you with:

- *the courage to be*
- *the courage to know deeply the divine design of your life*
- *the passion for the possible, and*
- *the willingness to bring this possibility into time and being.*

You are more than you think you are,
and something in you knows it.

Jean Houston

Gail Haile developed a way to make mesmerizing photo mandalas.
See them in color at http://hailefinephotography. com/ - /mandalas

WHAT STARTED IT ALL

In 2009 I started a Creativity & Camaraderie Club for myself for some pretty simple reasons:

- I needed something to look forward to each month. I was a middle-aged woman with a recently emptied nest who had just buried her mother and seen her husband through a cancer scare. I was not looking for another hill to climb.

- I was looking for ways to refresh my spirit and re-engage in a new phase of my life.

- I wanted to have more fun.

- I did not want to wait for the occasional vacation. I wanted fun built into my life. Here and Now!

- I wanted to meet and mix it up with some new people and age groups. I wanted those people to be right in my own community, not met only occasionally at out-of-town workshops.

- I wanted to increase my sense of community, to bloom anew where I was planted.

- I wanted to be encouraged, affirmed, and held accountable to play, take creative risks, finish "intended" projects, and "do something different" each month. I don't know about you, but I can dream and procrastinate forever!

I had already experienced the dynamic, enlivening, and healing power of well-structured groups in my professional life. I wanted to give that to myself for a change, so I did what I know is the first step in dream realization: take your dream out of isolation and team up with an ally and a cheerleader. I called my longtime friend and colleague, Jan Ferris, LCSWR, and asked her to have lunch with me. I told Jan my idea and she lit up. Her response?

"I really need something like that in my life right now. I've been wishing for the same thing!"

We were soon to learn this would be the overwhelmingly common reaction. When I researched existing "creativity club" formats to follow, I found none. Jan and I put our heads together and envisioned a successful, ongoing, committed group. Between the two of us, we had 45+ years of experience as psychotherapists and group leaders. We listed the structure and group ground rules we knew from experience help create, protect, and sustain a lively group over time.

Patricia O'Connor models one of the Christmas hats made by Ginny Palusky and a fleece scarf made by Nancy Zumpano at our holiday celebration.

WILL ANYONE WANT TO DO THIS WITH ME?

Step number one in breaking creativity barriers is to stop worrying what other people might think and be willing to show them what you have thought of. Even though I knew this, it still felt risky to send out invitations. I told myself, "I'll be lucky if I can get four people who will really want to commit to this. " To increase my chances, I sent out thirteen invitations. I was thrilled and amazed when 100% of the folks to whom I had sent invitations responded positively. Four of them then had to decline, but not because they did not want to come. Their work schedules simply would not permit frequent enough attendance to create group cohesiveness. With the nine enthusiastic "Yes please!" responses we received, plus Jan and myself, our group of 11 has held steady for the past four years. People even plan their vacations around it so they don't miss the fun. We have become a community of encouragement and joy. We can't wait to hear how each member has lived more fully each month.

RSVP: YES PLEASE! WHY PEOPLE WANTED TO JOIN OUR GROUP:

I was really excited with the whole concept. I felt like a thirst had been quenched. I accepted because I have been looking for ways to be accountable, to balance my life outside of work. I also was excited about trying something new. Nancy Zumpano

Right before I got your invite, I had realized that I needed to have more networking in my life and some new friends. I felt like I had created this group because of that intention... "Law of Attraction"! Patricia O'Connor

How did I feel about receiving this invitation? Happiness, relief (I needed this!). Excited anticipation. I felt honored (wow, I get to be part of a cool group of women creating something great together!). I accepted because I was hungry for all of it. Judy Wolf

My first reaction was an emphatic YES! I work in a creative field but work by myself and often feel isolated. Periodic meetings with other photographers helped a bit in terms of techniques and business, but did little to spark the core creative fire. Online networking with other photographers didn't provide any depth. The idea of gathering in person with other people for the purpose of sharing and encouraging creativity answered a longing that was being neglected. Even beyond the creativity aspect, I realize that it met a longing for personal contact that was also not being met. Gail Haile

It was just exactly what I'd been thinking of (some like minded people getting together around creativity). I was thrilled that you took the initiative and that we hashed it out together. Our creativity group is a central part of what makes my life feel so alive and relevant. It's the kind of "fun" I like to have the best... better than any cocktail party or shindig that I could attend. Jan Ferris

How did I feel when I got this invitation? Perfect timing! Then, OMG! What will I do that's creative? And every month? I was relieved to have the initial "prompts" that were sent. Then I thought, THIS is going to be a FUN adventure! Barb Trevvett

I was thrilled to be invited into this group. I love groups of supportive women – they have always been a lifeline for me and the idea that it would be focused on living more creatively made it even more appealing. Vige Barrie

The Hunger for Meaningful Community

We are not meant to be alone, we are meant to be parts of bigger families, bands, and tribes. Human beings want and need intimate support … Don't settle for nuclear family contraction. Extend!   Andrew Weil

If you desire a more meaningful, thriving life you must seek to get it together, in community with others. Abundant research shows that rich, affirming relationship networks:

- protect and improve your physical health
- increase your sense of emotional wellbeing
- help you live longer and happier

Research also shows that the type of social network matters.

- Authentic, respectful communication helps us; superficial chatter does not.
- Supportive "live body" presence and connection heals us and actually improves measurable health markers.
- Excessive reliance on the Internet and social digital media is actually increasing our sense of isolation, loneliness, and depression.
- Tangible human touch heals and uplifts us. A "cyber poke" does not. Feeling needed, feeling that we matter to someone, feeling that someone is expecting us helps us to thrive.
- Having trusted confidantes, even a therapist, improves our sense of well-being and health.
- Negative relationships create negative health and emotional consequences.

A COMMITTED CREATIVITY GROUP FEEDS A DEEP HUNGER IN THE HUMAN SPIRIT.

We need supportive community to encourage ourselves to:
- see ourselves more clearly
- expand beyond our habitual perceptual "ruts"
- take risks
- weather life more graciously
- come out of our creative "closets"
- come into authentic fullness of being

It's fun. It's fulfilling. It's uplifting. It generates goodwill, good humor, hope, and enthusiasm. It's good for your emotional and physical wellbeing. What's not to like?

If this speaks to you, I encourage you to identify someone you think might want to co-found a group with you. Try to identify someone whom people seem to naturally respond to and trust easily. You might consider contacting a well-respected therapist or minister to partner with you. Perhaps there is someone at a local art center, wellness center or library. Take them out to lunch. Bring this book with you. Brainstorm a possible invitation list (see Chapter 3). You will change many people's lives for the better and have a lot of fun doing it. The ripple effect over time can be amazing.

We do not find the meaning of life by ourselves alone - we find it with another. "
Thomas Merton

TEN BENEFITS OF A CREATIVITY & CAMARADERIE CLUB

1. Increase your sense of physical and emotional health. Research supports this and also suggests that regular positive social interaction is the happiness equivalent of feeling like you have increased your income!

2. Expand your sense of identity beyond the day-to-day routines of job, personal history, and family roles

3. Increase and build a more diverse social network. As time passed, our group naturally evolved to realize we "had each other's back" should the sudden need arise for a ride to a hospital appointment, dog sitting, skill exchanges, etc.

4. Get out of your rut. The only difference between a rut and a grave are the dimensions!

5. Experiment with new activities and ideas. This builds new neural pathways that help keep cognition flexible and intact. It makes you happy and builds increasing confidence.

6. Cross-fertilize each other with an amazing array of shared workshop possibilities, podcasts, DVDs, websites, articles, and ideas as enthusiastic group emails fly around.

7. Exercise your risk-taking muscle, and have more fun doing it.

8. Actually do some of those things you have only thought about or procrastinated on. *My favorite definition of procrastination? Passive-aggression against yourself!*

9. Experience being deeply appreciated and received by a supportive group. Learn how to give that to others.

10. Become more aware of inner psychological habits that limit your ability to take creative risks or to enjoy the diversity that exists in any group of human beings. Participating in any group offers us the opportunity to bump up against our own habitual psychological issues. Typical reactions that you may observe and conquer within yourself by consciously committing to an ongoing group are:

    • "compare and despair" thoughts
    • "I'm not good enough"
    • "I don't really belong here"
    • jealousy
    • judgmental and critical thoughts
    • competitiveness

When people do not create they become ill. Perhaps not sick in body, but certainly in spirit. Creativity is a lot like excrement. It needs to be excreted from your psyche on a regular basis or it poisons you. That is the absolute truth. Whatever your creativity is, shoveling snow or caring for a child, you must do it. You must do it on a regular basis. You must be using your life, living your life, from your creative center every day. If it backs up it hurts and pollutes you.   *Clarissa Pinkola Estes*

WHAT HAPPENS IN A CREATIVITY & CAMARADERIE CLUB MEETING?

We gather together once a month. Our group takes turns hosting in our homes. That has been part of the fun for us, and the "good vibe" feeling left in your house lasts for days. It has been a great way to get to know each other and see how our homes are expressions of who we are. . . from the simplicity of a cabin to a luxury bed and breakfast. If you are organizing a creativity club at work, art center, or another setting, the identified meeting place may be there.

We begin with a potluck. At first we thought this would simply be "healthy finger-food appetizers," but it quickly evolved into an eclectic feast. Eating together is a great icebreaker and bonding experience. We never co-ordinate our pot luck, and part of the flexible fun has been anticipating this great meal each month.

"Show and Tell" is next on the agenda. We take turns offering what we have done, what we are researching or preparing to do, etc. We are expected to bring concrete evidence of this to pass around: completed works, brochures, "before and after" photos, poems, PowerPoint presentations, knitting, etc. Sharing time is limited to a certain number of minutes per person. We are kept on track by the person appointed as the Time Keeper for the evening.

After each person has completed their show and tell time, we go around the group, and the group takes turns validating and affirming the person who has spoken by simply sharing one or two words that resonated in them as they were listening. (For a list of typical things we say, see Appendix D.) We actually discourage full sentences. Of course, they do slip in enthusiastically! A word or two of validation may sound insufficient, but trust us, it is very powerful over time. It is extremely rare and precious for someone to experience being profoundly received and then simply validated. This kind of brief, simple validation:

- protects participants from unwelcome commentary or analysis
- prevents the group from getting sidetracked and going off on tangents
- equally distributes the group's attention and focus
- helps to contain the meeting within the allotted time

We consciously manage the time so that everyone gets her "fair share" and so we can end the evening on time.

We determine where we will be meeting next month.

A significant part of the Creativity & Camaraderie Club vibe is the flurry of emails that go around the next morning as people express the energy, encouragement, and inspiration they are still experiencing the next day.

WHAT HAPPENS AS A RESULT OF MONTHLY MEETINGS AS SIMPLE AS THIS?

Take a look at Appendix B to see what one group of 11 women did in just a 36- month period!

BETTER THAN A BOOK CLUB?

Don't get me wrong. Many Creativity & Camaraderie Club members also are committed members of ongoing book clubs. It is our Creativity & Camaraderie Club, however, that gives us permission and support to make time to explore our own passions, curiosity, and interests.

YES, BETTER! HERE'S WHY:

- You will be encouraged to support and share your own creative actions rather than simply study or react to the ideas and creative efforts of others.

- You will be invited and supported to play in your own life

- You will be encouraged to shift out of "mental mode." A book club meeting is often about analyzing. A Creativity Club gathering is about encouraging tangible, embodied acts of "experimental enthusiasm" that up the ante of your own life.

- You will be exposed to a wide variety of stimulating interests, creations, resources, and ideas.

- You will experience what it feels like to receive unconditional support. There is no need to be anything other than who you really are. This support is created by closely following the recommended structure and group ground rules found in Chapter Four.

- You will undo old beliefs that you are "not creative."

- It's like being in "show and tell" in grade school with only your best friends in the classroom!

- A Creativity Club is about actively participating in your own life and being inspired and celebrated along the way by generous, loving people who are doing the same thing.

- You will be motivated and held accountable to explore what it means to take creative, "wholehearted" action in your life. Every time your group meets you will hear someone say, "If it weren't for the fact that I knew we were meeting this week, I would not have pushed myself to get this done!"

- The momentum of a Creativity Club inevitably spills out into creative engagement with the larger community. This book is an example of that! (See Chapter Eight: The Ripple Effect)

Spending time with friends is fun, but it may also yield a multitude of long-term physical and emotional benefits. Studies show that healthy relationships make aging more enjoyable, lessen grief, and provide camaraderie to help you reach personal goals, among other things. Maintaining positive relationships should rank up there with healthy eating and exercise as a necessary investment in your health. A number of studies have highlighted the importance of friends and good relationships to health. ...Being social boosts your immune system. Happiness is catching. Building a circle of friends makes you happy. The friends you choose make a difference. Madeline Vann

BUT IS THIS SELFISH?

> *I've learned lately that no one is going to hand me a permission slip and tell me to take time out for me.* Wynonna Judd

In a world full of problems and social inequities, some are concerned that taking time for themselves to focus on fun and creative projects is frivolous and self-centered. I assure you, this is not the case. Until you are grounded in your own inner creative wellspring, you will not have access to the energy and inspiration to serve the world whole-heartedly through your particular gifts. (See Chapter Eight: The Ripple Effect)

Give yourself permission to luxuriate in the support of a safe and encouraging creative team. After a while, you may notice there is a natural evolution that leads to creative acts that benefit the larger community. On the other hand, perhaps your "day job" already has a major focus of facilitating and helping others. Joining a Creativity & Camaraderie Club can help restore balance to your life, give you permission to play and refresh your spirit so you are then better able to serve.

> *Healthy connections with other human beings that are mutual, creative, energy-releasing and empowering for all participants are fundamental to women's psychological well-being.* S. Covington, Ph. D & J. Surrey, Ph. D.
>
> *Groups run by women are our psychic turf; our place to discover who we are, or who we could become, as whole independent beings. Somewhere in our lives, each of us needs a free place. A little psychic territory. Do you have yours?*
>
> *Gloria Steinem*

A love of nuno felting was discovered by Barb Trevvett

2

A Flexible and Generous Definition of Creativity

Living creatively doesn't mean only artistic creativity... It means being yourself, not just complying with the wishes of other people.

Matt Groening

Judy Wolf often experiments with creative embodiment.
She took a flying trapeze class...three times!

A Flexible and Generous Definition of Creativity

> *Art (creativity) is who we are, and what we do, and what we need. Creativity is not a result, it's a journey. The challenge of our time is to find a journey worthy of your heart and your soul.*   Seth Godin

Don't let the word creativity scare you! A successful Creativity & Camaraderie Club encourages and applauds a very broad definition of creativity. Your group's purpose is to give permission for everyone to indulge in simple acts of self-expression and desire "just because you feel like it." Make your creativity club more successful, dynamic, and interesting by expanding your definition of creativity.

A creative approach to life simply means that you are open to innovation, to change, to play, and to considering a new perspective.

Creativity Requires No Artistic Ability

It is a willingness to experiment, to explore, and to expand your comfort zone. It is a determination and personal commitment to "get out of the box" you have been confined in . . . or at least permit yourself a bigger box!

We define creativity as anything you do to interrupt your status quo, break free of confining habits, and give yourself permission to experiment and do something simply because it appeals to you to try it.

The purpose of a Creativity & Camaraderie Club is to encourage and support living more consciously in any arena important to wellbeing. Naturally, some group members' creativity will take traditional creative forms, e. g. , writing, painting, knitting, music, dance.

Be aware, however, that your urge for creative action may not be in an area we typically consider "art. "

Could you have a little more fun with your hat? Patricia O'Connor does!

THE SIX ARENAS FOR CREATIVE WHOLEHEARTED LIVING

Creativity is not just for artists. It's for businesspeople looking for a new way to close a sale; it's for engineers trying to solve a problem; it's for parents who want their children to see the world in more than one way.   Twyla Tharp

A Creativity & Camaraderie Club exists to encourage and applaud playful experimentation in all the many areas of balanced, wholehearted living. What does this look like? Club members come to meetings claiming all kinds of "creative living acts" in any of the six major arenas of wholehearted living.

1. ENGAGE WITH THE NATURAL WORLD, YOUR PHYSICAL ENVIRONMENT, AND YOUR EMBODIED SELF

- Give yourself a French manicure or pedicure for the first time
- Hike on a new nature trail
- Build a raised-bed garden and plant garlic
- Make gourd birdhouses and hang them throughout the yard
- Spend time gardening
- Take a flying trapeze class
- Refresh your office decor
- Go kayaking in a new spot
- Glue colored glass stones all the way up the base of a stairwell
- Remodel your kitchen
- Purge your house of excess stuff and clean out that closet
- Act as the general contractor on a major building remodel. Make handcrafted doors, mantelpiece, etc.

- Learn how to operate a backhoe
- Go rafting down the Grand Canyon
- Commit to a 40-day yoga practice
- Go on a 10-day cleansing fast

2. Experiment with Social Connection and Community

- Send old-fashioned snail-mail letters to let important people in your life know that they are just that —important. Decorate the envelopes!
- Volunteer to coach a seven-year-old's basketball team (while simultaneously learning how to play basketball on YouTube!)
- Create and offer book study groups on happiness and mind-body-spirit issues
- Take "Flat Stanley" photos to stay connected with a nephew in another state
- Join and support the creation of an artists' co-op
- Create a hooked rug as a wedding gift
- Make a five-year-old's birthday party special by learning how to make balloon animals
- Accommodate the upheaval that happens when an adult child needs to be welcomed back home
- Host "Integrative Energy Technique" trainings
- Ask for help five times in one month—Radical!
- Host a showing of "Happy, The Movie"

3. GIVE YOURSELF PERMISSION TO PURSUE PASSION AND DESIRE

This means allowing yourself to try things "just because you felt like it. " No justification, approval or permission is required. Allow yourself to be a beginner. Celebrate everything from the sublime to the ridiculous!

- Buy a "grow your own mushrooms" kit
- Take a watercolor class
- Attend a "Drawing on the Right Side of the Brain" workshop
- Take a trip to Spain
- Create live performance art pieces including a skirt made out of newspaper
- Attend nuno felting workshops and make scarves, birdhouses, wraps, and more
- Let others help re-vamp your wardrobe, introducing styles and colors that are new to you
- Take a cell phone photo of your shadow every day for a month Look every day for images of circles in your environment, take a photo and make a slideshow of them all, then make a Snapfish poster with the photos
- Buy a mandala coloring book and color the mandalas in it
- Research and create a family history book with stories and photos
- Make a soup recipe book as a gift after experimenting with 20 new recipes
- Learn how to create photo mandalas, and teach others how to do it
- Join Pandora online so that you can expose yourself to a greater variety of music
- Attend SolarPlate printmaking workshops
- Give yourself a "play day" to paint
- Research and learn how to tile a mantelpiece

4. EMBRACE AND EXPAND YOUR EMOTIONAL INTELLIGENCE

- Attend a series of SoulCollage workshops
- Explore a process called the "Pathwork Lectures"
- Sign up for an online "inspiration a day"
- Decide you actually have limits and begin to set better interpersonal boundaries: practice saying "NO" at least once a day for a month, keep track of this in a journal
- Practice slowing down and not striving so much
- Practice saying "YES" more
- Realize that "your schedule is your life" and take steps to do less and "put yourself on the schedule!"
- Schedule play dates with others
- Consciously engage in the challenge of caring for loved ones who have serious health challenges. Practice compassion for yourself as part of that challenge, because of all it requires physically, emotionally, and time-wise.

5. HAVE A VOICE, EXPRESS YOURSELF

- Take a Natural Singer workshop
- Write poetry and share it with the group
- Create a website to promote your "Creativity Retreat Bed & Breakfast"
- Have a show of your watercolors
- Do illustrations for a book
- Create a line of greeting cards using your own photography
- Dare to hang your own artwork in your home
- Write and promote a book on creating community
- Start a non-profit that sells your photographs for a major fund-raising campaign for equine-assisted therapy
- Give lectures in the community on compassion

- Create a website and start a blog
- Offer your mandala bookmarks for sale online
- Begin a "legacy letter" project for your grandchildren
- Offer monthly "moving prayer" qigong meditation in the community
- Enter a photo in an international competition

6. STRETCH YOUR INTELLECT, INTUITION, AND SPIRITUALITY

- Listen to Italian language tapes
- Experiment with a "divination-a-day" practice using several different divination sets
- Keep track of your dreams
- Make "themes for the year" on New Year's such as: "radical self-acceptance" or "everything is okay just as it is. "
- Commit to a daily meditation walk
- Commit to a daily spiritual reading
- Actively work on grounding to "stay in body"
- Start a daily mantra chant practice
- Go on a 10-day silent retreat
- Take an online course at www. spiritualityandpractice. com

Give yourself permission to get the most out of your life. If you're spending all your time scrubbing corners with a toothbrush, you're kind of missing the point.
Sandra Lee

PRIORITIZE PROCESS OVER PRODUCT

We discourage assessing and critiquing the product someone brings to the meeting. We do not jump in and suggest how they might have "done it better." Instead we celebrate and applaud the process of showing up each month to report how we have allowed ourselves to participate more fully in the desires of our own life, no matter how small.

Through witnessing each other's experiments, we are inspired and encouraged to give ourselves even more permission to explore. We encourage playful experimentation.

We welcome, relish, and celebrate the sublime and the ridiculous!

Inspiring the next generation, Tracey Lazore shared mandala making with her nephew. An example of "social creativity" celebrated by our club.

WELCOMING ALL STAGES OF THE CREATIVE CYCLE

Make your creativity club more successful by realizing creativity is not a linear process. Make sure your club honors and celebrates the creative cycle in all its stages. Expect people to attend each meeting no matter what phase of the creative cycle they are riding that month. Showing, telling, witnessing, and encouraging each other's creative acts are dynamic and contagious. They help you keep moving forward and give you permission to become even bolder in what you attempt.

THE CREATIVE CYCLE

INCUBATION PHASE = "PERCOLATION"

People come to group at times and say "I wasn't able to do anything this month. " They then proceed to talk about:

- last-minute googling of possible future workshops they may want to attend
- books they got out of the library to research how to make a raised-bed garden or how to tile a mantelpiece
- trips to a museum or craft store just to roam around for inspiration
- turning off the car radio for a whole month to "hear myself think and figure out what I want to do"

These are all important actions taken as part of the creative cycle, and it is important to see these as legitimate "offerings" to share at a monthly meeting. The Creativity & Camaraderie Club group helps name and celebrate this: "Wonderful! You are incubating something! Great! We can't wait to see what comes out of that for you!"

Preparation Phase = "Anticipation"

People may sometimes be hesitant to come to a meeting because they feel they have not completed what they want to do. It is very important that they come to the meeting anyway! Understand that the power of the group is that it helps celebrate this as a normal part of the preparation phase of the creative cycle. People have come to meetings showing:

- yarn they have bought for an intended sweater
- new watercolor paper they want to experiment with
- the paint chips they have found for an intended project
- art center and craft camp brochures and catalogs they have sent away for
- photos of the desk space they have uncluttered
- tickets bought for a trip or a concert
- bulbs they bought and intend to plant

These are significant actions. The group celebrates and acknowledges that. "You are taking action steps to get out of your rut, pursue a desire, and keep yourself moving. Yeah!"

ILLUMINATION PHASE = "CREATION"

A Creativity & Camaraderie Club exists to cheer people on so they actually act upon, and realize their desires or inspirations, no matter how small or diverse they may be. "Show and tell" is an opportunity to shine the light on the evidence of creative acts people have actually completed each month. I can't tell you how often we have heard, "I never would have done this if it weren't for the deadline of this group each month!" We find that the inspiration of what we witness each month stays with us, enriches our lives, and "ups our ante."

CONFIRMATION AND VALIDATION PHASE = "CELEBRATION"!

This is the heart and power of a successful creativity group. Built into the Creativity & Camaraderie Club structure is the practice of compassionate witnessing and encouraging validation. (This is explained fully in the Group Structure chapter.) During each person's "show and tell" time, they are listened to and received without interruption. Group rules prohibit attempts to advise, "fix," or "educate" aspects of another's experience or creation. The experience of being fully and respectfully received is very rare. To then hear affirming remarks on how our presentation inspired and affected others is extremely validating. We feel seen, heard, accepted and appreciated. It "ups our ante" and we are ready to attempt even more creative or outrageous acts by our next meeting.

Ginny Palusky performs her Thanksgiving rap song in her amazing newspaper skirt.

3

Gather Your Allies

A dream you dream alone is only a dream.
A dream you dream together is reality.

John Lennon

Relationships with others are the physical and
spiritual basis of creative energy. Nothing is further
from the truth than the popular notion that we create
alone and in isolation from the world.

Shaun McNiff

This sculpture was Lisa Miller's first attempt at playing with clay.
How do you know you "can't" if you never try?

WHERE TO FIND LIKELY CANDIDATES

It is hard for me to imagine a setting that would not benefit from starting a Creativity & Camaraderie Club. It fosters uplifting enthusiasm, creative thinking, and risk taking, and is a great way to enhance social connection and team spirit. Natural host settings or groups where you may find likely Creativity and Camaraderie Club candidates might be:

- at-home mothers
- retirees
- empty nesters
- menopausal mommas
- single people
- people in recovery
- after-school clubs
- counseling centers with a positive psychology focus
- community art centers and museums
- art stores and craft stores
- YMCA/YWCA
- libraries
- workplaces
- spiritual centers and churches
- wellness centers
- retreat centers
- bookstores

Your first creative act in forming a Creativity & Camaraderie Club is being willing to look "outside the box" for your possible candidates.

Give yourself permission to expand beyond any predictable social habits you may be stuck in. There are times in life when a new infusion of people and connections can really enliven you. This is an opportunity to mix it up a bit with new faces, age groups, and backgrounds. Diversity of age and backgrounds in a group make for a more dynamic and interesting mix. While you will certainly have some of your familiar friends on board, also seek to build into your group the opportunity for some new "cross-fertilization" of personalities and talents.

First Find an Ally

Create your group with an ally who is equally enthusiastic and committed to helping form and maintain a group. You will encourage each other in your determination to maintain a successful ongoing group over time. You may have to stick your neck out and interview several people over lunch before you find someone who feels like a dependable, enthusiastic ally with whom to co-found a group. Someone who has already demonstrated skill at facilitating people, or who you know people trust would be a great choice. Once you have formed an agreement with that person, you can brainstorm together a list of possible candidates to invite. Your ally will bring a bigger and more diverse pool of possible candidates from which to draw. You may find a local therapist, minister, teacher, professional personal coach, art center, library, or wellness center that wants to partner with you.

BE BRAVE, FIND YOUR TRIBE

As you brainstorm likely candidates, are there people you have admired from afar, someone you have always wanted to meet? Are there people with creative skills you would love to witness up close? Are there people you are aware of who are at natural "forks in the road" (empty nesters, newcomers to town, recently widowed or divorced, recently graduated)? Let your intuition and synchronicity guide you. Stand up and say, "Follow me!" Find the people who yearn for this and amplify their dreams. If you run into naysayers, don't let them stop you.

WHOM TO INVITE, WHOM TO AVOID

Your mother was right. Who we hang out with has significant effects on our mood, body, and potential transformation. So why not hang out with energizing, life-affirming people?

It really is important to think carefully about the individuals who might compose your group. Take your time and do this very intentionally.

Protect your enthusiasm from the negativity and fear of others. Never decide to do nothing just because you can only do a little. Do what you can. You would be surprised at what "little" acts have done for our world. Steve Maraboli

GOOD CANDIDATES

A good candidate will have some of the following qualities (or at least have the capacity and willingness to develop them):

- ability to keep a commitment to make the monthly group meeting a priority in their life
- ability to arrive and depart on time
- sense of humor
- determination to enjoy life more fully
- ability to listen respectfully to others without interrupting
- willingness to experiment with new experiences and behavior
- ability to hold the confidences of the group
- ability to happily celebrate the good fortune and talents of others
- authentic, thoughtful, genuine presence
- curiosity
- open-heartedness and generosity
- self-awareness

Our group initially formed with a mix of "already artists" and creative "wannabes". We had a watercolor artist, two photographers, a potter/glass artist, and a poet. Their motivation to join seemed to be the accountability to actually continue making their art and the encouragement to do so. The rest of us wanted the permission and accountability to actually give in to our yearning to live more creatively and wholeheartedly. We certainly have! (See Appendix B)

People to Avoid

Obviously and unfortunately, there are some people who simply will not make good group members if you want your group to thrive and survive. Think very carefully about this. One of the benefits of an ongoing group is that a lot of interpersonal healing can happen for people. However, proceed with caution. Your Creativity & Camaraderie Club is not an opportunity to attempt to change someone. You will need to eliminate people on your list who are incapable of learning to avoid the following behaviors:

- chronic lateness or "forgetting" meetings
- mean-spiritedness, criticism, pettiness or sarcasm
- jealousy, judgmental or competitive vibe
- whining, victim-oriented stance
- compulsive interruptions, poor listening skills
- unwillingness to maintain confidentiality
- invasion of personal privacy and boundaries
- unwillingness to respect group rules

Keep away from people who try to belittle your ambitions. Small people always do that but the really great ones make you feel that you too can become great.
Mark Twain

How Many Should We Be?

The recommended number for your Creativity & Camaraderie Club should be between ten and twelve. A group smaller than ten members can be hard to maintain and lacks the "cross-fertilization," dynamism, and diversity of a larger group. In order to avoid having too many participants, take a step-by-step approach. Send out just enough invitations and wait for the response. Then send out more invitations, if needed, to others on your list until you reach the desired number of committed people. An original group of ten to twelve will protect the longevity of the group, since over the years some people may move or need to drop out due to unavoidable life issues. If this should happen, you will still be left with a large enough group to be viable. A group that is too small may feel too inbred or confining over the years. Simply put, the lack of diversity is not as stimulating, liberating, or fun.

Traditional rug hooking is a creative and meditative passion
for Patricia O'Connor

The Invitation

> *Did you ever feel like the whole world was going to a party and your invitation got lost in the mail? Anonymous*

Here is the invitation we sent out. I recommend that you adapt and use it yourself. The more you let people know "what to expect," the more likely they are to engage in the idea. The quotes included in the invitation speak to a common hunger in many people and can help them recognize their own yearning.

I highly recommend sending your invitations by "snail mail" for greater effect. One of the benefits of an ongoing group is that it feeds the increasing hunger and need for tangible human interaction in an increasingly alienated and cyber world. Receiving an actual invitation in the mail sets the tone for this. Feel free to decorate the envelope! I printed my invitation on nice ivory paper using fonts that looked like a formal wedding invitation. The length required printing on both sides of a single sheet. You may want to mention this book as a resource. That way people are encouraged to explore the idea and familiarize themselves with the Creativity & Camaraderie Club structure, including ground-rules and resources, prior to your first meeting. The book can be found easily on Amazon or at www. danupress. com

SAMPLE INVITATION

Mary F. Mathews & Jan Ferris

*cordially invite you to consider becoming
a member of our Creativity & Camaraderie Club*

The structure is simple:

Agree and commit to meet one evening a month...we are aiming for the 2nd Wednesday of each month as a regular rhythm.

For the first meeting, consider some kind of creative act inspired by any one of the following prompts: Green, Fold, Key, Polka Dot, Connect.

Come to each monthly meeting having created something even remotely inspired by any one of these prompts OR come prepared to share anything that demonstrates you have taken some kind of creative action that enhances your life.

Participate in a group "show and tell" of playful creativity.

Bring a simple healthy appetizer to share. (I will have teas and water.)

What's the point?

All work and no play make Jack a dull boy.

"Where two or more are gathered"...there is more fun!

Get your creative juices flowing. This is about playful creativity, not high art. Anything goes! It may be as short and simple as a decorated haiku, a poem, a craft, a collage, a painting, a collection of quotes gathered, presented and shared somehow, photography, digital artwork, essay, inspired music mix, etc. , etc. , etc. It could even be that if the prompt word is "Green," you come to the meeting reporting that you were inspired to try a new spinach soup recipe. But you must come to the meeting with "evidence" that you did indeed engage in some creative activity.

What life have you if you have not life together? There is no life that is not in community. " T. S. Eliot

Far too often, people think that creativity is restricted to artists... Creativity shows up in our play and our improvisations. It spins out into the ways we relate to others, handle difficulties, and find innovative solutions to the world's problems. It is evident in the crafts we make and the hobbies we pursue. "Every person," according to potter M. C. Richards, "is a special kind of artist and every activity is a special art. " Frederic and Mary Ann Brussat

Come gather round for the inaugural "show and tell" Use any one of the prompts...or invent your own!

First Meeting Wednesday, May 3, 2009 6:00 – 8:30

(address)

RSVP: (email) (phone number)

Please remember to include your email address if that is comfortable for you

ARE YOU A GOOD CANDIDATE?

You are a good candidate for a Creativity & Camaraderie Club if you:

- meet the criteria of "Good Candidates" listed previously, or are willing to change and learn how to become one
- already have a creative passion or yearning, but find you are not making the time to make it a priority in your life
- think you don't "have an imagination", but wish you did, or feel you are "not creative", but really wish you were
- want to overcome interpersonal habits that have limited you in the past
- hunger for regular interaction with a dynamic, supportive community
- want life to be more fun
- desire to live more wholeheartedly

If you feel intimidated at the thought of risking a group experience like this, do yourself a favor. Watch or listen to every free podcast and TED talk, and read all the books by Brene Brown. She unlocks the mysteries of shame and vulnerability that keep us prisoner in boxes that are way too small for us. (See Appendix A: Online Resources)

4

The Structure That Holds it All Together

Build for your team a feeling of oneness,
of dependence on one another,
and of strength to be derived by unity...
Individual commitment to a group effort - that is
what makes a team work, a company work,
a society work, a civilization work.

Vince Lombardi

An Adirondack basket workshop helped Nancy Zumpano create a wonderful gift.

THE STRUCTURE THAT HOLDS IT ALL TOGETHER

The most essential ingredient of a successful Creativity & Camaraderie Club is the structure that holds it all together. A successful club will follow a consistent, reliable framework. Do not fall into the trap of equating "creativity" with an "anything goes" group anarchy. Save the spontaneity for the inspirations and creations you bring to show the group. A dependable structure is essential if you want your group to survive and thrive over time.

- A reliable group structure encourages more regular attendance and reduces the dropout rate.
- Structure fosters a sense of interpersonal safety and respect. These qualities are crucial to group cohesiveness, particularly when you are gathering relative strangers together.
- It allows authentic relationship to blossom and unfold over time.

While all this talk of "structure" may seem incongruously rigid for a group focusing on "creativity," trust us on this. Remember this: all of the childhood games you used to play had a set of rules and expectations to follow and they were really fun! The framework we outline is the key ingredient of fostering a successful group that thrives over time. Give yourself six months to experience this structure before deciding if it is working for you. Please replace any of your concerns about "rigid" with the word "respectful. " A group process that people experience as safe, consistent, reliable, and respectful will give your group the solid foundation it needs to form an ongoing rich, joyful, supportive community for many years.

TAKE ADVANTAGE OF OUR EXPERTISE

The following structure and group ground rules were developed by two psychotherapists with a lot of experience knowing "what works" for forming healthy group dynamics and protecting the future of a group. These guidelines keep your meetings moving, upbeat, and balanced.

Choose a day of the week and a time frame that will never vary. Our group meets on the second Wednesday of every month, 6:00-8:30. When someone cannot make a meeting on a given month due to a conflict, do not fall into the trap of offering to change your day to accommodate them. Keep them "in the loop" by emailing them a summary of what was shared that they missed. Your meeting cannot be a moving target if you want it to survive.

Begin promptly! Expect people to have arrived and settled themselves prior to start time. Do not delay start time for chronic stragglers.

Potluck takes place during the first half hour. The group "show and tell" begins promptly one-half hour into the meeting, always.

The order of sharing is pre-determined by a spontaneous "luck of the draw" process that the host initiates as people arrive or during potluck. This randomly created, pre-determined order of sharing prevents the group from falling into patterns based on personality dynamics that can create imbalances over time that diminish the culture of the group.

Each person is allotted a specific number of minutes for their sharing and feedback. This depends on the number of people in the group, and the length of the meeting. The time keeper volunteer in each session, or the host, is responsible for keeping track of this.

Always end on time. People will drop out of your club if they cannot depend on getting home at a reasonable hour. You will find you need to re-establish this rule from time to time. Once the enthusiasm and group dynamic blossom, it can be hard to bring the fun to a timely close.

We started off trying to set up a small anarchist community, but people wouldn't obey the rules.   Alan Bennett

GROUP GROUND RULES

Why do we need structure? Even jello needs a mold.   *Anonymous*

An agreed upon set of ground rules is essential when participating in a creativity group. It sets the stage for respectful emotional interaction, and creates a safe environment that supports learning, growth, and personal self-expression. This clear agreement creates a culture where we can support and nourish each other. This is a "sacred covenant" that will guide our behavior and help keep us on track. This is a commitment we make to ourselves and to one another. Make sure copies of the Ground Rules, the Compassionate Witness process, and the Hostess Responsibility Checklist are handed out at your first meeting, or that people have the book and review them prior to meeting.

This book was created to honor the years Patricia O'Connor has spent creating an artful garden. Fellow club member Gail Haile did the photography and together they planned the layout of the book.

MEMBER AGREEMENT:
AS A MEMBER OF THIS CREATIVITY & CAMARADERIE CLUB,
I COMMIT TO THE FOLLOWING EXPECTATIONS:

1.   I will make our monthly meetings a priority in my life.

2.   When unavoidable conflicts arise, I will notify the entire email list as soon as possible. Even when unable to attend, I will maintain my connection to the group by sharing via email what is "percolating" for me that month.

3.   I will arrive on time and leave on time.

4.   I will come to the meetings prepared to share something. I am aware of the different phases of the creative cycle, and will come to the meetings willing to share no matter what phase I am in: Incubating/Percolating, Preparing/Anticipating or Illuminating/Creating. Participating in validating and celebrating the creative offerings of others in the group is an action I take that encourages my own creative explorations.

5.   I will learn and practice the principles of Compassionate Witnessing during our meetings.

6.   I am aware that acclimating to the group structure may take a few meetings to feel "natural," and I commit to having patience and supporting the group creation in this way.

Learn the rules like a pro, so you can break them like an artist.   Pablo Picasso

How to Be a Compassionate Witness

Inspired by Dale Schwarz, M. Ed., ATR, LMHC
The Center for Creative Consciousness

Protect the right to confidentiality

Agree to keep feelings, thoughts, and experiences shared by the group inside the group "circle of trust." It is natural when working in creative groups to want to share your enthusiasm for the group process and experience. You can share your enthusiasm without revealing or identifying group members by name. "Wow, you wouldn't believe what this person in my creativity club did!"

Be accepting and non-judgmental

Agree to listen, observe and be present to the group without judgment, criticism, competitiveness, or comparison. This allows group members the support and encouragement to go forward in the face of self-consciousness and fear. With practice you will also become more able to turn the eye of the compassionate witness towards yourself! Do your best to simply listen open-heartedly. Allow yourself to observe what you can affirm and validate in each person's offering.

Allow only one person to speak at a time. No cross talk.

When you offer undivided attention, you hear what is being said, and the speaker knows they are being fully received and listened to. What a rare treasure in today's world! Being listened to with full presence and without interruption has often been cited as the most powerful and validating aspect of the group experience. Learn to respect others by limiting your urge to inflict your wisdom and expertise upon them. Avoid the compulsion to let your "helping hand strike again."

SUSPEND INTERPRETATION OF OTHER'S SYMBOLS, ART, AND EFFORTS.

Each person is their own authority on the mystery and meaning their images or creative offerings hold for them. What you think you "see" in another's work is usually a reflection of your own reality. (It can be very enlightening if you pay attention to that!) Allow each other to understand images and offerings without further "help" or "input. " The Creativity & Camaraderie Club is not an arena for evaluating with the mind of a critic or a therapist, but is a community of supportive celebration.

GRANT THE HOSTESS "GROUP LEADER" STATUS AND GIVE PERMISSION TO KEEP THE GROUP ON TRACK.

Without taking offense! Sometimes in the interest of time and group process, the group leader may need to interrupt to move things along or to remind folks to return to respectful group process ground rules.

DISCUSS BROKEN GROUND RULES.

The ground rules are likely to be broken sometimes. We agree that it is permissible, acceptable, and responsible to raise this issue. If you are aware that a ground rule has been broken and is creating a detrimental effect, you will help the group address it. Each member is fully responsible for keeping the covenant of the group circle. It is sometimes not easy to raise this issue, but it is a necessity if the group is to function at its highest potential and be a safe haven for all members.

Always be generous with praise and cautious with criticism. Applaud successes, and do your best to be a good listener   *Maud Purcell, LCSW*

WHAT OTHERS HAVE TO SAY ABOUT THE STRUCTURE

Silent, receptive, respectful listening keeps the group from becoming a counseling session.   Barb Trevvett

Managing the time element is important and becomes a long-term equalizer.
                                                  Patricia O'Connor

My friend attempted to start a similar group but did not instill the Ground Rules criteria. The group quickly devolved and now functions on a totally different basis. She is disappointed in the outcome.   Jan Ferris

I love witnessing and being witnessed! My life is so much richer due to this group and the "sacred space" the structure creates.   Judy Wolf

Although I am a reckless-creative at heart, I have learned in life that without structure things can quickly fall apart...I know structure can provide parameters to be equal, for all to be seen and heard. This is so important in the creative process and it is important for people to understand this.
                                                  Kathy Donovan

CHECKLIST FOR CO-FOUNDERS OF A CREATIVITY & CAMARADERIE CLUB

The initiating co-founders of a group need to anticipate that they will be "shepherding" the group through the first six months or so while the group culture is being established. After that, the group will have learned the structure and ground rules and should take "ownership" of the success of the group upon themselves so responsibilities are shared and a non-hierarchical vibe is maintained.

- ☐ The first two meetings should be hosted by the co-founders, who will model a meeting run on the recommended structure.

- ☐ After that, you need to be sure that the next hostess volunteer is identified before people leave at the end of the meeting.

- ☐ Hand out copies of the Group Ground Rules, the Compassionate Witness Process and the Member Agreement at the first meeting to anyone without a copy of this book.

- ☐ When your group is in the early stages and using prompts, you need to email everyone three potential prompts a month prior to the next meeting so people have time to work with them, if they desire to.

- ☐ After a meeting, send out a group email expressing appreciation for the prior evening.

- ☐ Five days prior to the next meeting, make sure a reminder email goes out reminding people of next meeting, and including the address, phone number, directions, etc. Ask for everyone to RSVP by group email, not just to you.

☐ If someone cannot make a meeting, group culture is enhanced when a group email acknowledging they will be missed is sent.

☐ When someone cannot make a meeting, a great way to keep them engaged and included is to send out a summary email the next day of what people shared that they missed. The co-founders will most likely be responsible for this throughout the life of the group.

☐ You may want to document the history of your group by taking notes on what people have done and taking photographs. It is amazing to review this later on!

☐ Feel free to contact me and send photos or summaries of what your group has been up to. I can post photos on the Creativity & Camaraderie Club Pinterest Board, and write-ups on my website or facebook page:

www. danupress. com

http://www. pinterest. com/mfmathews/boards/

https://www. facebook. com/StrategiesoftheSpirit?ref=hl

Checklist for Hostess Responsibilities

Hospitality means primarily the creation of free space where the stranger can enter and become a friend instead of an enemy. Hospitality is not to change people, but to offer them space where change can take place.   Henri Nouwen

After a number of months, the group will have relaxed into the structure and guidelines. It is then time for the entire group to take responsibility for its success. The "hostess of the month" runs the meeting at her house and keeps everyone on track, enforcing the group structure.

☐ A week prior to your meeting, the hostess of the month is responsible for emailing everyone to remind them of the upcoming meeting and to give the address and a phone number where she can be reached.

☐ If your group attendance is to be 10 or more on a given month, the hostess has the option of not preparing anything for the potluck. There will be plenty of food!

☐ The hostess is responsible for providing buffet set-up: plates, silverware, napkins, teas/coffee/seltzers, etc.

☐ The hostess determines how the group "show and tell" order will be determined for that meeting. This has been done in many creative ways, including:
  • a numbered divination card set or deck of cards from which people randomly draw
  • birthday dates
  • middle initial order

☐ The hostess is responsible for getting the meeting started on time and ended on time. The hostess can act as the time keeper unless someone else volunteers.

☐ The hostess is responsible for reminding folks to turn off all cell phones.

☐ The hostess provides a stack of "take home" containers or bags for all the leftovers people clamor for!

☐ The hostess makes sure that the next meeting place is agreed upon before everyone leaves.

☐ The hostess takes care of all clean up, so people can leave promptly.

The ornament of a house is the friends who frequent it.

Ralph Waldo Emerson

THE TIME KEEPER'S JOB

The common man is not concerned about the passage of time, the man of talent is driven by it.   Schopenhauer

The group determines how many minutes each person will have to share, depending on the number in attendance. Believe it or not, five minutes is really enough to be profoundly received and witnessed, with an additional three to five minutes to hear the group's validation words. We use a timer. When the timer rings, the person will hear it. The timekeeper's job is to gently encourage the person to come to a close, then to encourage the round of validation words. If someone begins to "over-speak" during this part of the process, the timekeeper gently reminds her that they have gone over their time limit.

Take care of the minutes and the hours will take care of themselves.

Lord Chesterfield

Seven Guiding Qualities of a Successful Creativity & Camaraderie Club

To affect the quality of the day, that is the highest of the arts.

Henry David Thoreau

1. Experimental Enthusiasm

We permit ourselves to try something "just because we feel like it." There is no need to "justify" or "explain" We get to simply "try activities on" to see if we enjoy them, without feeling the need to strive for expertise or make an ongoing commitment to it. We revel in "beginner's mind."

2. Unconditional Affirmation

A Creativity & Camaraderie Club exists to appreciate and affirm everyone's interests and explorations. Meetings are absolutely not about critiquing, evaluating, or analyzing what is shared. We applaud whatever and wherever folks are in any given month.

3. Unimpaired Curiosity

Anything goes! The whole point of a Creativity & Camaraderie Club is to encourage new explorations. Wondering what it might be like to try a flying trapeze class? Go on a 10-day silent retreat? Learn how to make mandalas in PhotoShop? Explore felting? Learn more about your digital camera? How will we know if we don't try it?

4. EAGER ANTICIPATION

The monthly meeting becomes something to look forward to. People have actually changed their vacation plans because they are so eager to see what everyone is up to each month.

5. ACTIVE ENGAGEMENT

A Creativity Club exists to encourage and hold us accountable so that we actually DO SOMETHING each month rather than simply fantasize or dream about it. Over time, even initially small actions build momentum with the tangible inspiration supplied by the group.

6. RESPECTFUL RECEPTIVITY

The Compassionate Witness process is an especially powerful tool. (This process is described thoroughly earlier in this chapter.)

7. ONGOING CELEBRATION!

The very essence of a Creativity & Camaraderie Club is the determination to:
- "show up" for yourself and others
- engage more fully in your own life, now!
- celebrate each other and yourself over the months and years

The real secret of success is enthusiasm.   *Walter Chrysler*

Shadow box art is just one of artist Ginny Palusky's many artistic pursuits!

5

Pot-Luckier Fun

If more of us valued food and cheer and song above hoarded gold, it would be a merrier world.

J. R. R. Tolkien

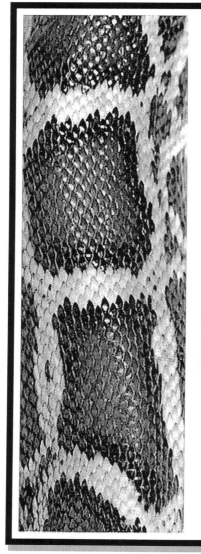

Boa

by Tracey Lazore

The full empty skin lies shed.
Patterns and markings still in place.

Do you think she felt it coming?
I think that she did.

An all over itch she couldn't scratch
or a suffocating tightness
she thought would never end.

I think that she did.

And that she welcomed the eternal second
of her soft, white underbelly
Splitting.
As in one breath, she glided away.
The same.
But bigger.

Poet Tracey Lazore often shares new poems at our monthly meetings.

POT-LUCKIER FUN

FOOD CREATES COMMUNITY

It's that simple. People are starving for the simple human dynamic that happens when we take the time to share a meal together. The potluck section of our meetings happens very quickly, during the first half hour. People arrive at the end of busy workdays bearing all kinds of offerings from homemade to take-out, sausage to popcorn. All sorts of delicious abundance quickly overrode my initial idea of "healthy finger-food appetizers." We arrive, set up the buffet, serve ourselves, take our seats, feast, and begin the meeting promptly one-half hour into the meeting time. No one in the group would trade this part of the meeting for anything. We do nothing to coordinate what is brought. We enjoy whatever shows up. Occasionally we get too many desserts. Oh well, somehow we bear it! The monthly food contributions are creative offerings in themselves. (For examples of some of the dishes folks have brought see Appendix E.)

WHAT WE NEVER SERVE

Although many of us in the group are well known to enjoy a glass of wine elsewhere, we never serve alcohol at our Creativity Club meetings. We strongly advise you to do the same. This sort of group is intended to be an incubator for raising consciousness and fostering the type of healing that profound presence can bring. That is the dynamism of our group. We remove any substance that lowers respectful awareness, curtails consciousness, or buffers presence. We exercise our risk-taking nerves without sedating them. We hope you will give yourself the same gift. Believe me, you will get so buzzed on the group dynamic and creative sharing, you will not miss alcohol at all.

Another practical aspect of this decision is that things can get pretty enthusiastic at a Creativity & Camaraderie Club meeting. Keeping respectfully to the ground rules that create and protect a successful group, and keeping the meetings within the time frame, can be much more difficult when inhibitions are lowered with substances.

As a group known to love a good time, I polled our group on this question. The unanimous and emphatic vote was that the group's success would be compromised if mind-altering substances were a part of it.

> *"There is such richness in the meal and the discussion. I feel strongly we would be cheating ourselves and each other of intimate presence if we included wine. "*   Jan

> *"I love a glass of wine as much as anybody, but I'm glad we've kept it clean and sober. We'd have made the mistake of thinking we were having so much fun because of the wine! We get intoxicated enough on each other's enthusiasm and creativity!"*   Ginny

If you choose to ignore this suggestion, and later find your group is not thriving, revisit this issue and the Twelve Sure-Fire Ways to Sabotage Group Success in Chapter Seven.

6

Developmental Phases of a Group

Coming together is a beginning.
Keeping together is progress.
Working together is success.

Henry Ford

Jan Ferris gives herself permission to take "art days" to play with paint. Will you?

Vige Barrie discovered she loves the freedom painting on Yupo paper gives her.

WHAT TO EXPECT AS YOUR GROUP MATURES

ENJOY EACH STAGE OF THE GROWTH CYCLE

Group dynamics develop and mature over time. Allow this to happen organically, naturally, at its own pace. The ease and intimacy within your group will be very different at your eighth meeting than it was in the first few. Expect this and accept it. If your group is a mix of relative strangers, you must allow trust to build over time. Be patient and keep following the group guidelines. The group ground rules provide a very predictable and respectful process that will foster group trust and increased risk-taking over time. The more your group commits to a culture of affirming and celebrating each other, the more quickly relaxed, joyful intimacy grows. Individuals vary on how long this takes for them. Hang in there. You wouldn't pull up a seedling that has just begun to sprout because the flower you hoped for hasn't arrived yet, would you?

STAGES OF GROUP DEVELOPMENT

INITIAL STAGE

Members are just getting acquainted with each other in this very important stage. They are testing the waters to see if the group is a safe, encouraging place to take creative risks and expose vulnerable doubts and insecurities. Members are getting used to the dependable goals, expectations, rhythm, and structure of the group. They depend on the organizing co-founders to make sure the group adheres closely to the direction the group guidelines provide. At this stage of group development it is vital to stick to the predictable structure and the culture of "affirm and celebrate." It is very important to respect personal boundaries at this stage and not push for more intimacy than someone is ready for. Consider the fact that people are returning to each meeting as solid evidence that something very good is happening!

Initially, the co-founders will bear the responsibility of tending the group to keep it on track and aligned with the guidelines. Once group members are familiar with the structure and a rhythm has been established, the group takes on ownership of its own success. For the first several months, one of the co-founders sends out a reminder email 4-5 days prior to the next meeting, asking for RSVP attendance for the next hostess. As the group matures, the next month's hostess assumes the reminder alert responsibility.

Within a day or two after a meeting, one of the co-founders sends an email with three potential "creativity prompts" for the next meeting. It is fun to see the incredibly diverse ways people use the prompts as springboards for their creative offerings. (See Appendix C for some possible prompts, or generate your own.)

WORKING STAGE

As a few months go by, returning members become increasingly free to anticipate and enjoy preparing for the monthly meetings. You may have no need for prompts after the sixth month. By now people are increasingly aware of their "wholehearted living" desires, large and small, sublime and ridiculous. The group welcomes and celebrates them all! If laughter is medicine, we are getting quite a healthy dose by now. We are regularly inspired by each other. Group emails often go around the day after the meeting to express enthusiasm and gratitude. Members begin to share resources, podcast recommendations, workshop opportunities, quotes, etc. A cross-fertilization of talents begins to take place as members become comfortable seeing the group as a resource for problem solving.

ANTICIPATING POTENTIAL CONCERNS IN EARLY STAGES: PROBLEMS OR OPPORTUNITIES?

As any group develops, you can expect that group members will be bumping up against their own psychological reactions to others. It is only natural. Participation in any group of human beings is bound to involve emotional dynamics, for better and occasionally for worse. Things will happen that trigger you. That is normal. You may observe yourself replaying "family-of-origin" issues or patterns of competitiveness, judgmental criticism, jealousy, self-doubt, or comparison. Experiencing this inner awareness is one of the great benefits of taking the initiative and risk to function well in a new group. Consider it all fodder for your own personal growth, an opportunity to experience and explore "I wonder what's going on with me?" One of our group members confesses now that she struggled with a powerful feeling at the beginning that she "did not belong." Now she is offering SoulCollage® workshops helping others to belong! Another member says that initially it was very hard to keep from "comparing and despairing" her efforts with others. Now she creates and shares her poems with abandon.

When the inevitable interpersonal irritations or concerns crop up, keep coming back to your commitment to "take the higher road" for yourself and others. Stay committed to your Higher Self and the wellbeing of the group. Learn to transcend anything that would undermine the morale of the group. After all, this will be your small arena for contributing to world peace. If ten people can't learn to "get over themselves," what hope is there? Hang in there, keep coming back to the Ground Rules. As you witness members' creative efforts over time, your heart will open and everyone's "inner stuff" will get refined in the process.

IMPORTANT: Your Creativity and Camaraderie Club is NOT a therapy group however, and NOT a place to have discussions about dealing with interfering psychological issues. For your group to succeed, you must keep its mission clear. The group exists to nourish, encourage, and celebrate any small actions taken to live life more fully. It is NOT an arena for psychotherapeutic conversations. Strangely enough, profound healing and happiness are increased in member's lives just the same!

Work with a wise counselor outside the group, if necessary, so that you can learn how to participate maturely in, and benefit from, a respectful group.

Mature Stage

At this stage, your group has really "jelled" into a "we" feeling. People are at ease with the structure and each other. A celebratory culture has been created. People accept and appreciate the differences in the group as a source of creative insight from which they can benefit. Everyone takes responsibility for the success and continuity of the group. Any issues are discussed and dealt with openly by group brainstorming and consensus. The group may have chosen a name for themselves...hopefully one that makes them laugh!

You may find that your monthly gathering becomes a network of social support beyond the group. What could be nicer than that? Our group has provided dog sitting, technical support with PhotoShop, photography and web-site development exchanges, rides to the hospital, meals when someone was down, etc. May it be so for you!

Below is an example of the sort of email exchange that may take place as you establish the group culture you are aiming to create in a Creativity & Camaraderie Club:

After one of our initial meetings, I was emailed by a group member stating she was "so very glad to have attended the prior evening, as her life had been very challenging on the personal front the prior month. "(She was coping with a difficult caregiver role for her beloved husband.) She mentioned that she had not talked about all of that stress in our group because she "did not want to turn our Creativity Group into a 'therapy group. '" I'm pasting in my response as we developed a "group culture" together:

> I am so sorry to hear of the challenges you are facing right now. . . and so glad if you find our Creativity & Camaraderie Club a respite from your caregiver concerns and the slings and arrows of life. That is exactly what I had hoped it would be. Yes, the Creativity & Camaraderie Club is NOT meant to be a therapy session group. . . but as we get to know each other the camaraderie part of it will, of course, include being authentic about ourselves and reference to our life situations. The majority focus, however, is meant to remain emphasizing the enduring part of ourselves. That part that continues to heroically engage in life through small creative acts, efforts, and good humor...the part of us that continues to appreciate and get support for the life we have left in us! It seems to me that the extra concerns of aging we face, the more we need it! It will be interesting to see how this develops. . . I suspect some intervening "course corrections" may be necessary as our group evolves. . . . right now I've heard back a couple of concerns that we've got to make greater efforts to have the group start and end promptly on time. Looking forward to seeing everyone next Wednesday!

Natural Cycles

There are natural cycles to everyone's life. This is true of groups as well. Your original group may meet for many years with most of the original members intact. Over the years some people may move, need to drop out due to unavoidable life issues, or find that the group's mission has helped move them to a new venture in their life. Should you find that your group is losing dynamism due to dwindling numbers, I encourage you to invite three new members all at the same time rather than just one individual alone. Please take the time and add new members very thoughtfully. All existing group members should be included in the process of considering and inviting potential newcomers. Do not mention the possibility to an outsider that they might join your group without first having discussed it thoroughly with all your other group members. Potential candidates must be enthusiastically welcomed by everyone. Sometimes there are professional or personal reasons why it would not be appropriate for a certain person to be included in the group. Understand that when you add new members to an existing group you are really creating a whole new group dynamic. You are really forming a new group. There will be an adjustment period. You may need to mourn the loss of the former group's personality for a while, while at the same time welcoming the fresh experience and dynamism that meeting a new group of people will bring.

Our Group's Experience

As our group anticipated our second and third-year anniversaries, we discussed how we wanted to celebrate. A field trip? Go out to dinner? After much enthusiastic brainstorming, we gradually realized, "What could be better than what we've been doing already?" No one wanted to have a month go by without the creative sharing. No one wanted to substitute "normal" free-for-all social conversation for the intimate presence and individual witnessing our group provides. No one thought dinner out at a great restaurant could be more fun or delicious than our random and eclectic potlucks. Everyone felt that the very best way to celebrate was to keep doing what we were already doing.

As we entered our third year of meeting, we realized that by witnessing each other's creative life yearnings, we felt we knew each other more intimately than is often possible even after years of "regular" socializing. At the same time, we also realized that we really knew very little about each other's personal history. That is actually one of the great benefits of a Creativity & Camaraderie Club. It is a place where you introduce yourself first through your current life yearnings and creations. It is a place where "who I would like to be and become" is more important than the standard answers that limit my identity to my past history (what do I do for a living? how many marriages/kids have I had, etc.)

As we entered our third year together, we thought it was time and might be interesting to learn more about each other. How do we do that? Creatively, of course, as part of our group meetings. Sometimes we now decide the monthly order of sharing by writing down an answer to a question the host has determined. We put the answers in a pot, and when an answer is pulled out of the hat, the group tries to guess who it is. (DO NOT do this during the initial stage of group formation, as it may feel too intrusive or personal.)

What sorts of questions have been asked?

- What was a nickname you had as a kid?
- If you could be mentored by any great historical, political, literary, theatrical or artistic figure who would you like it to be?
- Write down something from your past you don't think the group knows about you.
- If you were a car, what kind would you be?
- What motto would sum up your outlook on life?
- What task do you actually enjoy doing that many others find a bore or a chore?
- What is a memory that makes you feel really happy?

Coming up with a fun answer and trying to match each of them with the person who wrote it has now become part of our fun. We learn a lot about each other this way.

We cannot tell the exact moment a friendship is formed; as in filling a vessel drop by drop, there is at last a drop which makes it run over; so in a series of kindnesses, there is at last one that makes the heart run over.   Gloria Naylor

7

Protecting Group Boundaries

It's a slippery slope, Carrie. Without boundaries,
you never know what might happen.

Miranda, "Sex and the City"

Nancy Zumpano is triumphant after her first triathlon:
creative embodiment in celebration of her fiftieth birthday.

PROTECTING GROUP BOUNDARIES

The wellbeing and longevity of your group will be protected by staying alert to things that can deteriorate the culture of affirmation, celebration, and group cohesiveness. Expect that from time to time you may need to initiate a group "pow-wow" to brainstorm and respectfully address things that may threaten group intimacy, enjoyment, and boundaries. Our group does this by always including everyone in group emails and brainstorming as a group when questions arise so all voices are heard.

It is necessary to be alert to dynamics that can deteriorate the culture of affirmation, intimacy, and creative engagement you are building in your group.

TWELVE SURE-FIRE WAYS TO SABOTAGE GROUP SUCCESS AND LONGEVITY (THE "KISSES OF DEATH"):

1. Have your meeting day and time be erratic and varying.

2. Don't keep to a crisp start time.

3. Allow your meetings to run on long after the agreed-upon end time.

4. Don't insure that sharing time is distributed fairly.

5. Tolerate ongoing habits of late arrival.

6. Tolerate a lot of cross-talk during an individual's sharing time.

7. Tolerate a lot of unsolicited interpretation or advice regarding what someone has shared.

8. Have a group member who regularly comes without any intention of participating in the creative action requirement. Someone who just comes for the socialization of the group or as a voyeur.

9. Foster a culture of gossip between group members about each other outside the group. My definition of gossip? Talking about someone who is not present in anything but an affirming, understanding or supportive way.

10. Foster a competitive atmosphere rather than an atmosphere that celebrates everyone's process with equal appreciation.

11. Allow your group to drift into a culture of "therapy talk" rather than maintaining the focus on sharing and celebrating our current creative engagement in life.

12. Welcome outsiders to randomly attend group meetings. Sound unfriendly? Trust us, it disrupts the momentum and evolving intimacy of a group. It interferes with the "sacred circle" you are building. Don't do it if you want your group to thrive. (See Chapter Eight: Responding to Outside Interest)

8

The Ripple Effect of Creative Living

Every life needs a purpose to which it can give the energies of its mind and the enthusiasm of its heart. Start by doing what's necessary; then do what's possible and suddenly you are doing the impossible.

Saint Francis of Assisi

Lisa Miller stayed up all night in barns to photograph thoroughbred foals being born. Then she started the non-profit <u>Foal Project</u> to benefit equine assisted therapies. She has raised more than $50,000 to date! She has also become a fashion photographer! <u>http://www.lisamillerphotographyny.com</u>

THE RIPPLE EFFECT OF CREATIVE LIVING: HOW LIVING WITH
MORE ENTHUSIASM CAN CHANGE YOUR WORLD

Your group will eventually lead to creative acts that benefit and affect others in your family and in the larger community. It is inevitable. The group's continued affirmation, encouragement and support give us permission to "up our ante" and undertake larger visions and risks. What might this look like? Within three years members of our small group had done the following for the larger community:

- had a gallery show of watercolors in her community

- had a gallery show in her community of new photo mandalas.

- hosted a community showing of "Happy: The Movie"

- offered "Art & Empowerment with SoulCollage®" workshops http://www. artandempowerment. com

- hosted a Fresh Air Fund child

- coached basketball for seven-year-old boys (while learning the fundamentals of the game herself online!)

- attended printmaking workshops as a shared passion with her significant other

- offered a series of "Dangerous Old Women" SoulCollage® workshops

- created and offered a six-month study group called "Taking Happiness Seriously"

- retired early to be fully present to her partner in cognitive decline (while simultaneously renovating her house!)

- hosted art play dates with grandchildren, nieces and friends

- offered an "Energy Hygiene Basics" workshop

- participated in the 90-mile fund- and awareness-raiser "Ride for Missing Children"

- volunteered for Hospice

- promoted her workbook, Fall in Love With Your Community http://communityworkbook. com

- created a digital program that transforms personal photos into mandalas that encourage meditative play http://www. HaileFinePhotography. com

- established an online store for her fine-art note cards http://www. HaileFinePhotography. com

- raised funds to give all the graduating high school seniors a copy of the book *365 Thank Yous* by John Kralik

- offered a monthly "Moving Prayer"/Qigong hour for her community

- helped to create and open an artist's co-op http://artisanscorner.blogspot. com

- raised funds for Imagine: a Global Initiative for the Empowerment of Women http://www. imagineprogram. net

- hosted intuitive art workshops and energy healing trainings at her bed and breakfast artists' retreat

- wrote this book

- started the Strategies of the Spirit Blog: Integrative Wellness Practices for Wholehearted Living http/::www. danupress. com:strategies-of-the-spirit-blog:

RESPONDING TO OUTSIDE INTEREST AND ENTHUSIASM

Enthusiasm glows, radiates, permeates and immediately captures everyone's interest.   *Paul J. Meyer*

If your experience is anything like ours, when others hear about your Creativity & Camaraderie Club, they will inevitably say, "I want to belong to a group like that!" and "Can I come, please, please, please?" The best way to respond to this outside interest is to first encourage anyone interested to read this manual so they can understand the group structure. We strongly advise that you do *not* casually invite "visitors" into your precious monthly meeting. That may seem unfriendly and ungenerous at first. Please trust us on this. This suggestion is based on our professional experience and expertise with group dynamics. The success of your club depends on creating a sacred circle, a predictable structure, and a safe community. You are building a transformative community. (See the Protecting Group Boundaries section in Chapter Seven.)

Please do, however, find ways to generously respond to outside interest! You can respond to others enthusiasm by offering to be a visiting "mentor" for a few months as they establish their own group. Someone from an already established and successful Creativity & Camaraderie Club could attend the first four to six meetings of a new group to model the group process and keep folks on track. The mentor's time might be honored by having each member of the new group chip in $5. oo to $10. oo each toward a gift card or gas card.

Perhaps you could host an annual get together of your local area's Creativity & Camaraderie Club tribes?

The goal of a Creativity & Camaraderie Club is not to become an exclusive "secret society", or to create an "insider/outsider" vibe. These recommendations are based on the psychological factors that help sustain and protect group longevity. Protect the integrity of your group so that you can infect the larger community with your enthusiasm, and help others start groups of their own.

Boundaries are important for defining any 'thing'. A shape without a boundary is not a complete shape. When you have a boundary you have a thing. And when you have a thing, you can name it. It hence gains identity and meaning. The same is true of social groups, which makes their boundaries important. With a weak boundary, others can enter at will, pollute the culture, subvert the purpose and challenge the leadership. Paradoxically a strong boundary means the interior can be relaxed and friendly.

http://changingminds. org/explanations/groups/boundary_management. htm

I draw circles and sacred boundaries about me.   *Friedrich Nietzsche*

Judy Wolf experiments with watercolor...and many other things!

9

Jumpstarting a More Creative Life

An artist is an artist before they have ever produced a single thing...the production of something is not what makes one an artist. It's the soul that makes an artist, the center of the psyche that fills the person with creative fire...

If the person has the soul of an artist, the fire and the burning (as each and every individual does), they are entitled to the title of artist, before they have produced one single thing.

Clarissa Pinkola Estes

These hand-colored mandala and quotation bookmarks were made by Jan Ferris
and treasured as gifts by the rest of us!

DARE TO DABBLE, DABBLE TO DARE

To live a creative life, we must lose our fear of being wrong.

Joseph Chilton Pearce

Your Creativity & Camaraderie Club is a support team that gives 100% permission to play and experiment. While some of your members will already be experienced artists, writers, dancers, singers, knitters, or craftspeople, a typical group will also certainly invite and attract the "creatively wounded. " Your group is a safe place for people recovering from crippling messages such as "I can't draw," "It's only your imagination," "I'm not creative," "That's not practical," and "Who do you think your are, anyway?"

Consider giving yourself permission to be a dilettante and a dabbler. Give yourself permission to return to the un-pressured mentality of the sandbox for quite some time. You may need to allow yourself many months of experimenting with whatever strikes your fancy, without thinking you need to "get good at it. " That is how children learn what they like best, by following what attracts them and dropping what no longer holds their attention. If you have never had the opportunity to do this, your Creativity & Camaraderie Club is the place to get restorative affirmation, encouragement, and support. Have fun with this, and allow your group to celebrate your experiments with you. You may discover a hidden talent in the process, a new technique that enhances your craft, or an interest you had never considered before. A friend of mine took up beekeeping as a hobby!

Your Creativity & Camaraderie Club becomes your monthly deadline to take creative action. Your group understands that, and every attempt is to be celebrated as you build a creative life.

It goes without saying that insisting you must make your creations "expert" takes all the fun out of it! Your Creativity & Camaraderie Club gives you permission to simply play, to do something "just because you feel like it." Your group will diffuse your fears and perfectionism by sharing and showing you how they overcome their own. Your group will be a safe place to laugh at your vulnerability. Members have arrived at meetings with enlarged copies of doodles they did while attending business meetings, with poems created by randomly selecting refrigerator word magnets, and an invented recipe for quinoa pizza salad.

Sometimes, after dabbling for a while, you may find that you are increasingly attracted to dig deeper into one area for creative action. Your Creativity & Camaraderie Club will be a gold mine of networking, resources, and talent. Your dabbling may lead you to greater daring. Your daring will make you feel more alive and enrich everyone around you.

I know that without this group I never would have participated in the fiber-felting group that I now absolutely LOVE, LOVE, LOVE, because I never would have known that the class existed. That means that I would not have made my first felted scarf. Btw, I'm headed back to do more felting on Sunday!!!! Barb

Questions to Get You Going

Ask the right questions if you're going to find the right answers.

Vanessa Redgrave

The following questions were inspired by Michele Cassou's
Questions to Awaken Your Creative Power to the Fullest:

What would I create if my life didn't have to be perfect or impressive?

What creative living act would I take if no one were looking? If no one would ever know?

What would I do if I were totally free to do anything? Physically? Artistically? Musically? Craftily? Spiritually? Relationally?

What might I do if I did not have to live up to anyone else's expectations or even my own?

What is one thing I have thought I would do "If I only had time"? "If I could afford it"? "If I had talent. "?

Which people have I secretly admired or found myself thinking, "I wish I could have what she's having!" What is attractive about that? What life force does that person represent?

What act of creative living would I take if it didn't have to make any sense at all?

What would I create if I didn't have to be consistent?

What would I do if I could relax, loosen up, be spontaneous?

What act of creative living would I commit if I did not censor my intuition? My unexpressed inclinations?

What would I do if I were able to be playful?

What might I try if I had no desire or expectation that I had to become an "expert" in it?

What would I do if I wanted to play with changing the direction of my "usual" life?

If detectives were investigating my home, clothing in my closets, bookshelves, furnishings, refrigerator, car, what assumptions would they make about the person living there? Am I happy with those assumptions? Do they feel like "me"? What would I want to change?

What would I do if I were not afraid to change?

What do I just "feel like doing"? No explanations or justifications necessary?

Do I want to "balance" my life by creating in another arena of wholehearted living, or do I want to "exaggerate" an already existing interest?

Who would I be if I had the support of kind,
affirming, enthusiastic people cheering me on?

People who encouraged me to experiment,
to play, to take new risks,
and branch out in new directions?

Your time is limited, so don't waste it living someone else's life...have the courage to follow your heart and intuition. They somehow know what you truly want to become. Everything else is secondary. Steve Jobs

Note to Self: Rehearsing What You Truly Desire

You can't see clearly if your imagination is out of focus. Mark Twain

Research supports that the imaginary "rehearsing" of your most desired outcome actually increases the likelihood you will live into that result. This is an important part of sports psychology and performance enhancement. Olympic athletes, stage performers, and top public speakers know this. They regularly imagine and rehearse a successful desired outcome. Take advantage of this yourself by using the great free service at FutureMe.org. You will be using your imagination to set your intentions and rehearse desired outcomes.

Go to https://www. futureme.org and write a series of emails to yourself. Or, if you prefer texting, use the free app HiFutureSelf. Have these delivered on future dates that you select. Consider writing one weekly to keep yourself motivated and to hold yourself accountable to live into your most creative life intentions. Research shows that practicing excitement about the future and using your imagination to envision positive future outcomes increases those hopeful outcomes. The act of writing it down makes it more tangible, and engages more parts of your brain in setting your intention.

Dear Me:

I'm so glad you listened to your enthusiasm when you first heard of the Creativity & Camaraderie Club concept. Did you notice how your body got a charge of yearning and energy?

Isn't it interesting that as soon as you started to let yourself play with this idea, so many people who might make great creativity companions have crossed your mind? Now that your True Self knows that you are listening and are going to honor it, all kinds of creative ideas and yearnings are popping up. It's finally time to stop stopping yourself!

By now you have read the handbook thoroughly and have contacted someone you think will make an enthusiastic ally. You have a date to meet for lunch. I'm so glad you are doing this! It will be interesting to see where this takes us all!

Love,

My True Self

As part of her office makeover, Gail Haile decoupaged her office organizers with images from a trip she took with her daughter

10

Have More Fun,
Live More Wholeheartedly,
Encourage Each Other

What is life for? It's for you.

Abraham Maslow

You can discover more about a person in an hour of play than in a year of conversation.

Plato

Many club members express themselves through SoulCollage®,
a very accessible way to begin to dabble with creativity.
She Spins On by Mary Mathews

Have More Fun, Live More Wholeheartedly, Encourage Each Other

> *Ever since happiness heard your name, it has been running through the streets trying to find you.* Hafiz of Persia

Isn't it time you finally turned around to greet it? I wrote this book because I hope you will.

I wrote this book because I know personally and professionally that participating in a healthy, ongoing, committed circle inspires, enlivens, and transforms people's lives like nothing else can.

I have learned that simply looking into the past for individual healing is not enough. (It may be important and necessary, but it's not a complete recipe for a wholehearted life.) I have learned that no one comes into fullness in isolation. We need others encouraging us, hoping for us, and inspiring us. We need a safe community that will celebrate our successes, and sympathize with our frustrations. We need to go out and find or form our own tribes for the life we want to live now!

Women thrive psychologically when a safe, supportive circle of other women embraces them. Everything in modern culture would have us isolated or in competition with each other. We must consciously choose to create and participate in small committed circles of community to counter that. The transforming and enlivening power of this must be experienced to be believed! We discover ourselves when we have a safe place to share experiences, be witnessed and supported, laugh, cry, and learn from the role modeling of others.

Facilitating such circles has been the most rewarding aspect of my career.

I wrote this book because I know the hunger and need for this is out there, but the "how to" is not easy to find. Without guidelines and ground rules, the best-intentioned groups can devolve into a superficial coffee klatsch, or worse. An intentional group needs a center, an organizing principle.

WHY CREATIVITY & CAMARADERIE?

Simply put, I chose creativity as an organizing principle because it was the most fun! Creating a camaraderie group with a broad definition of creativity at its heart gives a lot of permission for experimentation. Why not let the power and benefit of your sacred circle unfold with enthusiasm for life as its organizing principle?

Your life will be refreshed by identifying your small inner yearnings and giving yourself permission to explore them in tangible ways. A group that shares and celebrates this is dynamic, fun, enlivening, profound, and transformative. What's not to like?

A sacred circle that supports you in exploring your curiosities, enthusiasms, and creative interests, will empower you in ways you have not yet imagined. I know that with the ongoing encouragement and support a Creativity & Camaraderie Club provides, it is inevitable that a positive effect will spread well beyond the boundaries of your group.

I want to encourage the formation of as many supportive circles of women, as soon as possible. When women gather in safe, encouraging circles they find their voices and their power increased.

The world really needs the wisdom of women now. Women need to support each other as we bring our creative energy forward. We need to be grounded in our own creative wellspring. Only then will we have access to the wholehearted energy and inspiration to serve the world better through our particular gifts. A Creativity & Camaraderie Club is an incubator for personal and community transformation. Let's have some fun on the way!

When we come together to play and be, we are truly ourselves. When we are truly ourselves it is wonderful. When we act collectively in that wonder we do transformative work for our community and our world. Brad Colby

I would love to hear what your Creativity & Camaraderie Clubs create together. Please let me know and help spread the joie di vivre virus!

www. danupress. com

pinterest. com/mfmathews/the-creativity-camaraderie-club-handbook/

www. facebook. com/stratetegiesofthespirit

Vige Barrie's watercolor and interior illustrations grace a book.

APPENDIX A: RESOURCES

CHECKLIST OF RESOURCES TO GET YOU GOING

If you have a great resource you think should be included, please let me know! (at http://www. danupress. com)

INSPIRATION FOR THE CREATIVE PROCESS

- ☐ The War of Art: Break Through the Blocks and Win Your Inner Creative Battles, by Steven Pressfield and Shawn Coyne An important book on what keeps us from doing what we want to do in any arena of our lives.

- ☐ The Creative Fire: Myths & Stories on the Cycles of Creativity, by Clarissa Pinkola-Estes CD or MP3 audio available at SoundsTrue. com

- ☐ Mastering Creative Anxiety, by Eric Maisel, Ph. D

- ☐ Questions to Awaken your Creative Power to the Fullest, by Michele Cassou

- ☐ The Buddhist Art Doctor: Prescriptions for Creative and Non-Creative Seekers, by Michele Cassou

- ☐ Do More Great Work: Stop the Busywork, Start the Work That Matters, by Michael Bungay Stanier, Seth Godin, Michael Port, and Dave Ulrich

- ☐ The Creative Habit: Learn It and Use It for Life , by Twyla Tharp

- ☐ The Millionth Circle: The Essential Guide to Women's Circles, by Jean Shinoda Bolen, M. D. If you want more encouragement on the power of participating in a committed, intentional group

- ☐ Art & Fear : Observations on the Perils and Rewards of Artmaking, by David Bayles and Ted Orland

- ☐ Spirit Taking Form, Making a Spiritual Practice of Making Art, by Nancy Azara

- ☐ Art Heals, How Creativity Cures the Soul, by Shaun McNiff

- ☐ Art is a Way of Knowing, by Pat B. Allen

- ☐ The View from the Studio Door: How Artists Find Their Way in an Uncertain World, by Ted Orland

- ☐ Free Play: Improvisation in Life and Art, by Stephen Nachmanovitch

PAINTING, DRAWING, COLLAGING, ETC.

- ☐ Drawing Lab: 52 Creative Exercises to Make Drawing Fun!, by Carla Sonheim

- ☐ Art From Intuition: Overcoming your Fears & Obstacles to Making Art, 60+ Exercises, by Dean Nimmer.

- ☐ Expressive Drawing: A Practical Guide to Freeing the Artist Within, by Steven Aimone

- ☐ Celebrate Your Creative Self: 25 + Exercises to Unleash the Artist Within, by Mary Todd Beam

- ☐ Painting form the Inside Out: 19 Projects to Free Your Creative Spirit, by Betsy Dillard Stroud

- ☐ SoulCollage® Evolving, by Seena Frost

- ☐ Collage for the Soul: Expressing Hopes and Dreams Through Art, by Holly Harrison and Paula Grasdal

- ☐ Mandala Designs, by Martha Bartfeld (a grown up coloring book)

- ☐ Totally Tangled: Zentangle and Beyond, by Sandy Steen Bartholomew (doodling on steroids)

- ☐ Drawing on the Right Side of the Brain, by Betty Edwards

- ☐ Zentangle Untangled: Inspiration and Prompts for Meditative Drawing, by Kass Hall

- ☐ Confident Color: An Artist's Guide to Harmony, Contrast and Unity, by Nita Leland

- ☐ The Complete Book of Gourd Craft, by Ginger Summit and Jim Widess

☐ Monotypes: Mediums & Methods for Painterly Printmaking, by Julia Ayers

☐ Coloring Mandalas 3: Mandalas of the Sacred Feminine, by Suzanne F Fincher

PHOTOGRAPHY

☐ Photographing Flowers, by Harold Davis

☐ Creative Close Ups, by Harold Davis

☐ 50 Photo Projects, by Lee Frost

☐ iPhone Photography Secrets, by Chet Davis. An inexpensive online course at: http://www. udemy. com

☐ Multiple books on digital photography and PhotoShop by Scott Kelby

GARDENING

☐ Gardening for a Lifetime, by Sydney Eddison

FIBER ART

☐ The Quilts of Gee's Bend, by William Arnett
☐ From Felt to Fabric: New Techniques in Nuno Felting, by Catherine O'Leary
☐ 500 Felt Objects, published by Lark Crafts

☐ Ravelry: a treasure trove of knitting inspiration and free patterns   http://www. ravelry. com

☐ Hook Me a Story, by Deanne Fitzpatrick

WRITING

☐ Writing Down the Bones: Freeing the Writer Within, by Natalie Goldberg

☐ Room to Write, by Bonni Goldberg

☐ A Poetry Handbook, by Mary Oliver

☐ Free podcast: Garrison Keillor's The Writer's Almanac for daily poetic inspiration http://writersalmanac. publicradio. org/podcast/

☐ Scrivener writing organization software http://literatureandlatte. com

☐ APE: Author, Publisher, Entrepreneur: How to Publish a Book, by Guy Kawasaki

☐ Local writers' support groups

☐ The Creative Penn website   (information and free podcasts on self-publishing   http://www. thecreativepenn. com/

WEBSITES FOR ART SUPPLIES, BOOK-MAKING, FLYERS, ETC.

☐   http://www. cheapjoes. com (art supplies)

☐   http://www. dickblick. com(art supplies)

☐   http://www. danielsmith. com(art supplies)

☐   http://www. snapfish. com(customize your own book)

☐   http://www. blurb. com(customize your own book)

☐   http://www. vistaprint. com   ("free" business cards, etc.)

OPPORTUNITIES FOR CREATIVE EMBODIMENT

☐   Trapeze School of New York
     http://newyork. trapezeschool. com/

☐   Zoar Outdoor in Western Massacussetts
     http://www. zoaroutdoor. com

☐   Ballroom dance weekends in the Catskills
     http://www. stardustdance. com

☐   Claude Stein's The Natural Singer workshops
     http://naturalsinger. com

☐   Canoe & Historic Train Ride outing
     http://www. adirondackrr. com/thendara. html

☐ Beaver Brook Outfitters in NYS (organized rafting, kayaking, fishing, snowshoeing, caving, etc.)
http://www. beaverbrook. net

☐ Cooking classes

☐ Kripalu Center for Yoga & Health
http://www. kripalu. org

☐ Local hiking clubs

☐ WOW: Women on Water (kayaking trips and water sports)

ONLINE CREATIVE INSPIRATION

☐ Free video TedTalk, "Your Elusive Creative Genius," by Elizabeth Gilbert
http://www. ted. com/talks/elizabeth_gilbert_on_genius. html

☐ Two free video TedTalks by Brene Brown on dealing with the issues of vulnerability and shame that can stop us from living more creatively and joyfully http://brenebrown. com/videos/

☐ Free 15-minute podcasts on creative obstacles related to our personalities
http://podcasts. personallifemedia. com/podcasts/227-joy-of-living-creatively

☐ Free podcast interview, "The Art of Noticing and Then Creating" with Krista Tippett and Seth Godin
http://www. onbeing. org/program/seth-godin-on-the-art-of-noticing-and-then-creating/5000

☐ Creative challenges, fun inexpensive classes and short-term online "art camps" for all ages and abilities
http://www. carlasonheim. com

☐ Mixed media classes
http://www. creativeclearinghouse. com/Online-Class-Reviews

☐ National Novel Writing Month event
http://www. nanowrimo. org

☐ Virtual school for artists by artists
http://camp. pikaland. com

☐ SoulCollage® process
http://www. soulcollage. com

☐ More information and inspiration on SoulCollage®
http://www. kaleidosoul. com

☐ Taking doodling to a whole new level
http://www. zentangle. com

☐ A great way to collect, organize and share your inspirations and creations
http://pinterest. com

☐   Articles on creative thinking and creativity resources
    http://www. creativethinkinghub. com/see-all-posts

☐   Extravaganza of creative prompts, mini-courses, etc.
    http://www. artellawordsandart. com

☐   The Center for Creative Consciousness
    http://www. tocreate. org

☐   Software tutorials for just about anything you may want to
    become more skilled at
    http://www. lynda. com

☐   Courses for many interests
    https://www. udemy. com

☐   TEDTalks (free online videos with great ideas to stir your cu-
    riosity)

    http://www. ted. com/talks

Workshop and Learning Venues

Please share your regional resources with me and I'll add them to a
list at: www. danupress. com

☐   The Center for Creative Consciousness (workshops and cor-
    porate and individual creativity coaching with Dale Schwarz)
    http://www. tocreate. org

☐   Local art centers, museums, and adult education sites

☐   Old Forge Art Center
    http://www. viewarts. org

☐ Snow Farm (summer arts and crafts camp for adults!)
http://www. snowfarm. org

☐ John C. Campbell Folk Art School
http://www. folkschool. org

☐ Zea Mays Printmaking Studio
http://www. zeamaysprintmaking. com

☐ The Printmaking Center of New Jersey
http://www. printnj. org

☐ Kripalu Center for Yoga & Health
http://www. kripalu. org/

☐ Omega Institute
http://www. eomega. org

☐ Touchstone Center for Crafts
http://www. touchstonecrafts. org

☐ Fletcher Farm School for Arts and Crafts
http://www. fletcherfarm. org

☐ Art New England: summer workshops sponsored by
MassArt
http://www. ane. massaart. edu

☐ Anam Cara Writer's & Artist's Retreat Center
Beara Peninsula, Ireland
http://anamcararetreat.com/

Appendix B: Creative Acts

Attended workshops on the following topics:
"Natural Singer"
mandalas
Integrated Energy Healing
intuitive painting
photography
watercolor
Drawing on the Right Side of the Brain
SoulCollage ®
SolarPlate printmaking
monotype
digital photography
NIA (neuromuscular integrative action)
photopolymer etching
trace-drawing monotype
PhotoShop
Portraiture

Group members also:
made computer mandalas
took a creativity retreat day
decorated a journal
brought a doodle notebook and pencils on business trips
changed house colors
attended "Happiness" conference with Brene Brown
made a quilted Christmas tree skirt
purged, redecorated, and remodeled
traveled to Rome, Italy
traveled to India
traveled to England
made a photo book

helped mother design a quilt
experimented with an art form called "quilling"
invented a pizza quinoa salad recipe
photographed a godson's graduation
witnessed a grandchild's birth
glued colored glass tiles up a stairwell footing
taught a computer mandala class
created clay sculptures
made pottery
took flying trapeze classes
made outrageous jewelry
painted on glass
got an agent for a memoir book project
went to Spain
made a photo-book to capture beautiful meditative garden
baked creative birthday cakes and cupcakes
made hooked rugs
tiled a mantelpiece
completed a "paint-by-number" (yes, they still exist!)
 grew mushrooms
enlarged doodles on photocopier
took a booth in a community festival to promote a workbook
celebrating community
took ballroom dancing lessons
made a five-foot pillar candelabra
made angel "prayer jars"
 experimented with Sanskrit mantra chanting
made mandala bookmarks with quotes and offered them online
introduced a five-year-old to camping
knitted a sweater for a grandchild
made nuno felted scarves
wrote an article including photography for Victorian Magazine
jet-skied on the ocean
salvaged and refinished "junk" furniture
hosted an intuitive painting workshop
zen-doodled a tabletop
made blueberry rhubarb rosemary jam

designed an I-Phone skin
started a non-profit for equine-assisted therapy
SoulCollage®, SoulCollage®,, and more SoulCollage®,
had a gallery show of original watercolors
did illustrations for a book and watercolor for its cover
made multiple fleece scarves
had a gallery show of large photo mandalas
took photos for David Cassidy's website
did daily morning "angel writing" meditation
played hooky from work for a day to play with a friend
created a music slideshow to celebrate a home remodeling project
hosted "grandmother weekends" organized around creative play
planned a "mystery trip" for husband with a "clue a day"
knitted a baby blanket
studied German
entered etching in sidewalk art show
made an Adirondack pack basket
practiced being patient
practiced saying "No!"
practiced saying "Yes!"
many wardrobe makeovers using Dressing Your Truth system
dyed clothes
felted a pocketbook
learned new computer skills
created websites
experimented with photography techniques
made a felt doll
cleaned out garage for a stained-glass studio
decorated a journal for friend
sewed cloth pocketbooks
engaged in drawing meditation process "Prayer in a Chair"
planned graduation trips to honor the young people in my life
made a soup cookbook on Blurb. com
nuno felted a banner of Our Lady of Guadalupe
did a gold and leopard wardrobe makeover
volunteered at Rescue Mission
volunteered at Hospice

painted a front door bright yellow
did the "three pages a day" practice from The Artist's Way
made a sparkly camera strap
bought a sewing machine, retailored outfits
took figure drawing class
wrote poetry
rebuilt manifold on hot water heating system
made a photo book on Snapfish
made beaded necklace
wrote haikus
rearranged furniture
participated in international "Threads of Grace" giving circle
honored longing for "non-striving" by doing less and "being" more
practiced asking for help each week
made Solarplate® etchings
hiked and rafted in the Grand Canyon
had photographs accepted for a national magazine cover
learned how to use a backhoe, drive a tractor, and run a brush hog
undertook landscaping projects
created CDs with "happy songs" as gifts
planted garlic for first time
created a luxury artist's retreat center

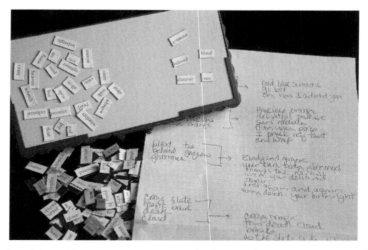

Synchronicity guides poet Tracey Lazore. She draws refrigerator magnet words at random and then writes out the wisdom she finds hidden within.

Appendix C: Prompts

Sample Prompts for Inspiration

You may want to consider offering three possible "prompts" each month for the first six months of your group formation. They are emailed out by one of the founding members four weeks prior to the next meeting, i.e. a day or so after your last meeting. Members may (or may not) use one of them as a springboard for creativity. It can be a lot of fun to see the diversity of how folks use the prompts as a creative springboard. Once your group is firmly established you most likely will no longer need them, although from time to time it can be fun to have a month when the group undertakes a unified prompt challenge again. There are an unlimited number of possible prompts. Add your own to this list! Those that follow are intentionally vague so that they could be developed in any direction, any medium, any which way:

green	structured
family	circular
polka-dot	linear
box	repetitive
wiggly	brown
black and white	eyes
spring	story
fluid	rhythm
hot	whisper
doodle	sound

envelop	birds
soft	re-use
light	lists
dark	things I see
sparkly	grateful
heart	
grow	floral
haiku	technology
hieroglyph	scenery
dreamy	"ZenTangled"

☐ Bookmark this webpage for remarkable lists of creative prompts:pinterest.com/rillaith/creative-prompts/

Grandson sleeps on a "long distance hug" pillowcase made just for him by Barb Trevvett

Appendix D: Affirmations

What Affirmation Words Sound Like

The affirmation words offered to each participant after their "show and tell" time are a most important part of the Creativity & Camaraderie Club process. While you will be tempted to speak volumes, trust us that "less is truly more" here. *Of course* our "words" do get wrapped in a sentence or two. We seek to simply speak words that attempt to capture our feelings as we witnessed the person sharing and how their efforts affected us. The safe process of being fully listened to, received, and affirmed is truly transformative over time. Notice that the hallmark of these words is that they are:

- celebratory
- appreciative
- affirming
- kind
- congratulatory
- encouraging

Here is a partial sampling of the sort of things said as part of the affirmation process. *Each of these was said with a big exclamation point afterwards!* Imagine them being said with a smiling heart.

vivacious	inner light
striking	adventurer
fertile	resilient
multiplier of blessings	determined
craftswoman	you are the hub of the wheel
rejuvenating	commitment
many-layered	integrity
rich	genuine

warrior for the light

contagious (in a good way!)

enthusiasm on steroids

va-va-voom

self-care

centered

inhabiting yourself

alive

full force

Indiana Judy

embodied enjoyment

courageous

true adventurer

legacy

profound

open

life task

eclectic artist

quester

thriver

clear channel

in the flow

living love personified

letting in wonder

grounded

sparkly

infectious (in a good way!)

vulnerable

aware

tapped in, tuned in, turned on!

muse with muscle

queen of loving

extraordinary

sacred trust

goodness

poetry priestess

appreciator

mentor

impressive

good steward

"inspiratrice"

freedom

generativity

precious

blessed

leader

percolating

joyful

animated

synchronicity

vivid

emanator

on fire

math missionary

priestess channel

gorgeous

stunning

elegant mirror

permission to be big

free

generous spirit

Vesuvius of creativit

Appendix E

Pot-Luckier Possibilities

A very partial list of the foods we have brought for pot-luck

(Note: We have learned that soups need to be served in doubled-up *small* paper cups to fit on plates. We have. also learned to have the host supply take-home containers for the leftovers people clamor for. Several people in our group are gluten-free, so remember to check with each other about food allergies.)

avocado soup

black bean soup

lentil apple soup

coconut squash soup

prosciutto & melon

sausage bites & mustard

broccoli raisin salad

caprese salad

fruit salads

green salad & pomegranate

avocado, cucumber, & tomato salad

Asian mushroom caps

quinoa couscous

strawberry, cucumber feta salad

eggplant ricotta casserole

marinated mushrooms

deviled eggs

ricotta spinach pie

brownies, brownies, & more

brownies

potato salad

homemade peppermint candy

quiche

orange, olive, & parsley salad

curried cauliflower

nut mix

7-layer Mediterranean dip

pizza quinoa salad

corn casserole

angel hair zucchini pesto

gummy bears

Swiss chocolate bars

roasted root vegetables

blueberry juice

cherry tomatoes

black bean sweet potato casserole

kale salad

Thai tofu, hazelnut, & rice
casserole
hot cheese dip
chicken legs with lemon and
garlic
caramelized onion & Gruyere
pizza
berry and apple crisps
ham
rice salads
Indonesian chicken
meatballs
Indian tofu
chicken tandoori
chicken boursin casserole
ricotta cake
sauerbraten
bean potato bake
salmon filet
chocolate-covered

strawberries
Chinese take-out
chicken riggies
greens
sauerkraut & sausage
popcorn
cheese plates & crackers
"better-than-sex" cake
carrot cake
cappucino cookies
savory turkey muffins
mushroom lasagna
snow peas & cherry tomatoes
pomegranate feta salad
spinach paneer
grandma's marinara
gluten free baguettes
grilled eggplant
spinach boursin
stuffed celery

Appendix F: Creativity Quotes

Quotes Too Good to Pass By

Living creatively is really important to maintain throughout your life. And living creatively doesn't mean only artistic creativity, although that's part of it. It means being yourself, not just complying with the wishes of other people. Matt Groening

The new meaning of soul is creativity and mysticism. These will become the foundation of the new psychological type and with him or her will come the new civilization. Otto Rank

There is a fountain of youth: it is your mind, your talents, the creativity you bring to your life and the lives of people you love. When you learn to tap this source, you will truly have defeated age. Sophia Loren

While we have the gift of life, it seems to me the only tragedy is to allow part of us to die - whether it is our spirit, our creativity or our glorious unique-ness. Gilda Radner

You must not for one instant give up the effort to build new lives for your-selves. Creativity means to push open the heavy, groaning doorway to life. Daisaku Ikeda

Always leave enough time in your life to do something that makes you happy, satisfied, even joyous. That has more of an effect on economic well-being than any other single factor. Paul Hawken

What we do now is to be valued, but we need to do more, so that it's more exciting to other people, and therefore that excitement shines back on us and we're able to have the energy to do more, to widen our creativity.

Siobhan Davies

To find a miracle you have to leave your comfort zone. You have to leave where you are. Take steps, allow yourself to leave the safety of where you are right now...Bless yourself, find out what unique gifts you have that will let you transcend the situation you are in.   Dr. Mona Lisa Schultz

I think creativity is spiritual. I absolutely believe that. F. Murray Abraham

Every person has the gift to imagine and join with the Divine in the ongoing creation of the universe. Every culture links creativity and spirituality. Music, dancing, poetry, and painting are common ways to express our soul and our delight in being.   F. & M. Brussat

Creativity is God's gift to us. Using our creativity is our gift back to God.

Julia Cameron

Practice means to perform, over and over again in the face of all obstacles, some act of vision, of faith, of desire. Practice is a means of inviting the perfection desired.   Martha Graham

Life is a series of natural and spontaneous changes. Don't resist them - that only creates sorrow. Let reality be reality. Let things flow naturally forward in whatever way they like.   LaoTzu

We are a culture of misfits — not because there is anything wrong with us as a people but because we are accustomed to becoming things we aren't. So we don't fit into our own souls. Our schools put out students to fit the economy, for instance, rather than the heart. Good thinkers go into accounting rather than philosophy because accounting pays more. Fine writers go into law because law is more prestigious. Young people with artistic talent go into computer science because computer programming or hotel management or engineering are full of "opportunities" — read "money" — that a water-colorist lacks. The problem is that when we do not do what we are clearly made to do we are doomed. We spend the rest of our lives looking for the missing piece of ourselves that we lost before we knew we had it. Then we wonder why the work we do bores us, no matter how many cars we have, no matter how beautiful the vacation house may be. We can't figure out why we still feel restless about life. We wonder what it is that isn't right: the schedule, the children, the marriage, the place. We lose a taste for life. Then, it is time go give ourselves the space and means to become again. We need to rearrange the furniture of life to make way for the essence of life: We need to set up an easel and paint. We need to start the woodworking we always wanted to do. We need to take the courses we always wish we had. We need to join the book clubs that talk about the things we are interested in discussing. We need to begin to knit and cook and write and garden. We need to do those unfinished, un-started, undeveloped things in us that ring the bell of bliss and authenticity. Then life will become life again and all the rust of it will wear away. When we become what we know ourselves to be, we will come home to ourselves. The rabbis put it this way: "Rabbi," the disciple asked, "what shall I do to be saved?" And the Rabbi said, "How should I know? Abraham practiced hospitality and was saved. Elias loved to pray and was saved. David ruled a kingdom and God was with him. Follow the deepest inclination of your heart and you, too, will be saved." When we live from the inside out rather than from the outside in, everything in life begins to fit.

Joan Chittister

Charter Members of the original Juicy People Creativity & Camaraderie Club

WHY DID WE NAME OUR CLUB JUICY PEOPLE?
WE WERE INSPIRED BY THIS QUOTE:

Hildegard of Bingen, twelfth-century mystic, counseled her spiritual directees to be "juicy people", folks who are so filled with wonder and curiosity, with lusty appetites and high sprits, that they embrace life, liberty and the pursuit of happiness with a burly, grinning bear hug. To be juicy is to be:

- *a fearlessly joyous optimist*

- *a trouble-maker tirelessly afflicting the comfortable*

- *a passionate lover of good talk and tasty food*

- *an anonymous prophet hovering over the cosmological riddle*

- *a frequent violator of the ordinance against indecent exposure of the heart*

- *and a guerilla in the insurrection against Dream Molesters everywhere.*

Rich Heffer

Juicy People are people who are aroused by life itself and engage in it creatively. We hope you'll join us! We'd love to hear what your groups have been up to, and what you have named your groups.... or feel free to use ours!

We look forward to hearing from you. If you enjoyed this book and have a moment to spare I would really appreciate a short review on Amazon. Your help in spreading the word is gratefully received.

Join us at:
www. danupress. com

pinterest. com/mfmathews/the-creativity-camaraderie-club-handbook/

Vige Barrie

Jan Ferris

Gail Haile

Tracey Lazore

Mary Mathews

Lisa Miller

Patricia O'Connor

Ginny Palusky

Barb Trevett

Judy Wolf

Nancy Zumpano

ABOUT THE AUTHOR

Mary F. Mathews, LCSWR has been a licensed psychotherapist for more than 20 years. She has designed, led, and participated in many encouragement group models. Her passion is to help enliven people by gathering them together to share their best selves. She is a SoulCollage ® facilitator, an Interactive Imagery Guide, and a Dream Interviewing Diplomate. As a DCEP for the Association of Comprehensive Energy Psychology her work includes exciting and embodied methods. She is a dynamic speaker and group facilitator.

Mary is a playful printmaker and a contemplative woods-walker. Her husband and her daughter are the wind beneath her wings...as is her little Norfolk Terrier.

She is the face behind Danu Press. www. danupress. com

DANU

PRESS

Artisan Publisher of Strategies of the Spirit

INSPIRE, ENLIVEN, TRANSFORM

27108464R00081

Made in the USA
Charleston, SC
02 March 2014